Sistine Madonna   *Dresden*

By Raphael

THE SPIRITUAL MESSAGE
OF
GREAT ART

THE SPIRITUAL MESSAGE
OF
GREAT ART

An Interpretive Study of the Life and Work
of Six of the Masters of Modern Painting

by

FREDERICK DOYLE KERSHNER, M.A., LL.D.

Dean of the School of Religion, Butler University

Edited by
JAMES MILLER

MEIGS PUBLISHING COMPANY
Indianapolis, Indiana

EDITOR'S FOREWORD

These lectures on the six great masters in Italian art were delivered under the auspices of The American Society for the Extension of University Teaching.

Dr. Kershner has sought in these lectures to discover the idea which the painter and sculptor tried to embody in their works. Here again the study is ideal in character. What stories do these Olympians of the brush and chisel tell? What thoughts do they express? What mysteries do they suggest? What glories do they reveal? What lessons do they teach? Do the ideals embodied in the works of the artists studied by the author reflect their character and their outlook on life? These are some of the questions Dr. Kershner answers.

The author studied his subjects from the originals in the various European collections and galleries, bringing to this first-hand study several years of careful training. In addition to these advantages, Dr. Kershner employed the talents with which nature has endowed him—an acute sense of beauty and proportion and the ability to interpret their embodiment in art. He has sought to find the meaning, as well as the beauty, incorporated in these great creations of human genius, and, with the scholar's reverence, has told what he found there. His lectures are interpretative studies of the greatest and most superb body of plastic art in existence.

JAMES MILLER

WASHINGTON, D. C. 7524

CONTENTS

ILLUSTRATIONS

It is the business of art to create an ideal world, in which perception, life, understanding, action, all elements of human life sublimed by thought, shall reappear in concrete forms of beauty.

—John Addington Symonds

LEONARDO DA VINCI

. . . . .

Painter of Life's Mysteries

LEONARDO DA VINCI

Leonardo da Vinci was the natural son of an Italian gentleman of rank, who lived in the castle of Vinci situated in the beautiful valley of the Arno, a river immortalized in the poetry of Shelley and Byron. His mother was a peasant woman named Caterina, of whom we know almost nothing. He was born in 1452, only a few months before the fall of Constantinople sealed the doom of the Eastern Empire. He was a precocious boy, brilliant and attractive, qualities which he preserved throughout a long and full career. While but a lad he puzzled his teachers with questions in mathematics and at the same time had such a genius for harmony that he could play the lute and improvise both verses and music which, an old chronicler says, was "little short of divine." He was tall and graceful and endowed with such physical strength that he could bend bars of iron, and yet his touch was so delicate that he became master of pencil and brush. At the age of eighteen his father took him to Florence and apprenticed him to Verrochio, the most famous sculptor of his time, and maker of what is regarded as the greatest equestrian statue in the world, the statue of Colleoni in Venice. Verrochio was also a painter, and one of the greatest teachers of his age. Not long after Leonardo became his pupil, Verrochio gave up his work as a painter. He was commissioned by the monks of the famous Vallambrosa convent, just outside of Florence, to paint a picture of the baptism of Jesus. Vasari relates that Leonardo, by request of his teacher, assisted in this work. He was assigned the part of painting an angel, a task which he did so well that it outdid everything else in the picture;

whereupon Verrochio was so much chagrined that he refused ever to paint again. The painting now hangs in the Academy of Fine Arts, Florence, and the angel, which is still pointed out as the work of Leonardo, is unquestionably the most beautiful part of the picture.

From the beginning of his career, Leonardo was attracted by the mysterious and the bizarre. Among his early work are two heads of Medusa, one of which, by his father's request, he painted on a shield. It is recorded that while he was at work on the latter picture he shut himself for several days in a room with toads, lizards, serpents and all manner of hideous reptiles, and when the picture was done it was so terrible to look upon that it seemed to be Medusa herself turning the beholder into stone by her horrible stare. Both of these Medusas are lost, but there is a Medusa head in the room adjoining the famous Tribuna in the Uffizi Gallery which is catalogued as Leonardo's, and which is great enough for the greatest painter in the world to have produced. There is about it a mysterious fascination that enchains and, at the same time, horrifies the mind. I have wandered by the Uffizi Gallery many times and have been drawn almost irresistibly into the room to look again upon this Medusa, a head as terrible almost as the one fabled to have been struck off by Perseus with the sword of Hermes. It can only be seen under a certain light, and is usually swung back from the wall that a better view of it may be obtained. The fiery breath, the livid skin, the awful eyes, the serpent hair, in all its green and gold magnificence, make such a combination of effects that the beholder can never forget them. The picture is small, about 2 by 3 feet, and has a number of famous paintings around it, among them, the *Calumny* by Botticelli, but it easily holds its own against any or all of them. Sometimes when the visitor first enters the room there is nothing to be seen but a patch of glossy black and gray, but as the

Head of the Medusa

By Leonardo da Vinci

Florence

light changes serpent heads appear and the monster, little by little, as it were, awakens to life. Shelley's poem on this picture well describes its fascinating horror and beauty which he calls "divine":

> "Upon its lips and eyelids seems to lie
> Loveliness like a shadow, from which shine,
> Fiery and lurid, struggling underneath,
> The agonies of anguish and of death."

At the age of thirty Leonardo left Florence for Milan where he lived for twenty years. Why he gave up Florence has always remained a problem. The story is told that he went as an ambassador from Lorenzo de Medici to the Sforza of Milan, and having played so sweetly upon a lute of silver, which he made in the shape of a horse's head, the Italian bandit, who ruled the Lombard city, was so charmed that he would not part with him. During these twenty Milanese years he produced nearly all of his greater works—*The Last Supper,* the Equestrian statue of Francesco Sforza, the prize picture made in competition with Michael Angelo, the *Battle of the Standard,* and part of the *Mona Lisa.* Great as these works were, and are, they are but few in number compared with the achievements of Raphael in a corresponding twenty years. There were two reasons for this: first, Leonardo's genius was so restless that it could never be satisfied with any external achievement, and second, he was such a brilliant courtier and so much in demand for other things that his hours were wasted in the daily routine of the court. Leonardo worked upon *The Last Supper* at intervals for ten years and then said it was not finished. He worked four years on *Mona Lisa* and left it unsatisfied with the result, declaring it was incomplete. The *Battle of the Standard* did not get beyond a cartoon, and even the Equestrian statue, many think, was never cast, the model alone having been completed. No greater testimony to the genius of this

supreme wizard could be given than the fact that with so few
productions of his brain and hand, common consent ranks
him with Raphael and Michael Angelo, both of whom produced so much more. After the fall of Sforza, Leonardo,
in 1502, entered the service of Caesar Borgia, son of Pope
Alexander the Sixth, and a skilful soldier despite his dissolute and disgraceful life. Leonardo became Borgia's chief
engineer, and devoted himself to scientific studies with as
much interest and enthusiasm as he put into art. Borgia
ruled about two years, and not long after his death Leonardo
left Italy for France where he died in 1519. The last period
of his life is marked by the production of his two Madonnas
in the Louvre and the only classical pictures he is known to
have painted, a *Leda* and a *Pomona,* both of which are now
lost, the former, as was usual with him, never having been
finished.

Very few facts of his life are known, but all of his biographers testify to his goodness of heart, to his extraordinary
brilliancy of intellect, which won for him the name of "Wizard," to his handsome person which combined the strength
of Hercules with the grace of Apollo, and to his deep religious feeling which made him shrink from attempting to
embody the Christ face in his pictures. A story, not well
authenticated, however, is told of his dying in the arms of
the French king who made a pilgrimage to his home in
Amboise. One of the most beautiful things recorded of him
was his devotion to his peasant mother, from whom he was
separated at birth but whom he never forgot. Though living
at the courts of kings and princes, and extolled as the greatest genius of Italy, he still found time to watch over and
care for this unlettered peasant woman and to soothe and
comfort her in her dying hours. How much of his mother,
often sad and unhappy, he put into the calm face and mys-

terious smile of *Mona Lisa* we do not know; perhaps more than we think.

That we may understand Leonardo's place in the world of art it may be well to survey briefly the progress of Italian painting from Giotto to the time of the High Renaissance. Modern painting dates practically from the advent of Giotto, the first great artist of the modern world, who was born near Florence, July 4, 1376. Instead of following the stereotyped forms and rules of medieval art, Giotto was taught by nature, and while but a child in many things pertaining to the technique of painting, he conveyed such a vivid sense of reality that, even to this day, his work is supremely fascinating. He put life and action into his pictures, and his superb dramatic touch made every painting a real story in line and color. The visitor to Italy who fails to see the Arena frescoes at Padua, where Giotto is seen at his best, misses something which is alone worth the cost of the trip. A hundred years later, Masaccio, in the Brancacci chapel at Florence, added an element at which Giotto had scarcely more than hinted, the element of characterization. Giotto told a story in a lifelike way, while Masaccio made the story element subordinate to the character element. The one is preeminently master of plot, the other of characterization. Both were true to life and nature. The Arena chapel at Padua with Giotto's frescoes, the Brancacci chapel at Florence with Masaccio's, the Sistine at Rome with Michael Angelo's and the school of San Rocco at Venice with Tintoretto's superb paintings are classed by Ruskin as the four supremely great art buildings of the world.

After Giotto and Masaccio, new possibilities in painting developed, the most important among them being that of movement in Pollajuolo, that of landscape and light and shade in Verrochio, Leonardo's teacher, that of ideality in Botticelli and that of the nude in Signorelli, the master of

Michael Angelo. As Giotto had made the story central in his work and Masaccio character, so Botticelli made ideas the central feature, striving to paint soul rather than body. Following these pioneers came the four supremely great names in Italian art,—Leonardo, Angelo, Raphael and Titian.

Leonardo had the dramatic power of Giotto multiplied many times, as the superb action of *The Last Supper* so tremendously reveals. Masaccio never even dreamed of such characterization as is portrayed in the *Mona Lisa* and in the countless sketches of da Vinci, who was also supreme in his mastery of movement, as the fragmentary copies of the *Battle of the Standard* sufficiently attest. His skill in handling landscape, light and shade is seen in the *Virgin Among the Rocks* and in the *Mona Lisa*. He did not devote his power to painting ideas, but when he touched that realm he equalled Botticelli at his best.

Dr. Richter catalogues only ten existing pictures which Leonardo painted or assisted others in painting. One of these is a picture of Verrochio's, which has been mentioned; another is the unfinished *Adoration of the Magi*. Of the eight remaining there is one in the Vatican, one, *The Last Supper,* at Milan, one in London (also a cartoon there) and four in the Louvre, Paris. This list, as will be observed, omits the *Medusa*. Twenty other pictures known to have been painted by him are lost. There are quite a large number of others attributed to him in various galleries in Europe but none of them can be said with any degree of certainty to be his. His four monumental works were his Equestrian statue, which was, in the opinion of most critics, the greatest statue of the kind in the world, his *Battle of the Standard,* painted in a contest with Michael Angelo, probably the greatest battle scene ever put on canvas, his *Last Supper,* regarded as the greatest single painting in existence, and the *Mona Lisa,* certainly the most celebrated portrait ever painted. Thus, in four distinct lines, Leonardo stands first, and it is because of this supremacy that he ranks as peer, if not superior, to Raphael and Michael Angelo, and this notwithstanding the paucity of his work as compared with the large number of theirs.

Leonardo was sixteen years in making the Equestrian statue, of which only the model seems to have been finished. It is said to have been twenty feet high and was set up in a public square in Milan in 1493, a few months after the discovery of America by Columbus. This statue commemorated the triumphant entrance of Francesco Sforza into Milan, seated upon his horse and carried upon the shoulders of the people from the gates of the city to the cathedral. Tall and thin, with broad chest and shoulders, a waist so small that he could span it with his hands, bluish gray eyes beneath shaggy brows, a sallow, discolored complexion, prominent nose and thin lips—this is the description given by historians of Sforza's personal appearance. A bandit, rough, daring, unconquerable, a sort of an Italian Cortez or Pizarro, he was a character well calculated to fire the imagination of Leonardo. What became of this statue is not certainly known, though twenty years after its construction it had completely disappeared, destroyed, according to a tradition recorded by Vasari, by the archers using it as a target when the French army sacked Milan in 1499. If this be true its destruction is another item in that colossal indictment, covering the ages, which art makes against the demon war.

The *Battle of the Standard,* like the Equestrian statue, is also lost. Only a part of the picture, copied by Rubens with due Flemish exaggeration, remains. It was the first great battle picture of the people of Florence or Milan. Fortunately, or unfortunately, there are not many great battle pictures. Perhaps the best known are to be found in modern French painting. The *Battle of Issus,* a mosaic from the ruins of Pompeii, is the most celebrated representation of ancient painting in existence, but is not in itself a great picture. The *Surrender of Breda,* by Velasquez, comes short of a battle scene. Raphael's *Defeat of Attila* does not equal much of his other work. David's *Sabine Women,* Gros' *Eylau* and the long series of scenes from the life of Alexander, painted by Le Brun, now in the Louvre, are great pictures, and well known, but not among the greatest. The *Battle of the Standard* gained the prize in competition with Michael Angelo, who was already famous, though at this time twenty years younger than Leonardo. This painting was to have been hung in the city hall, Florence, but it was never completed. The copy by Rubens, imperfect as it is, conveys some idea of Leonardo's power of representing action. While the *Mona Lisa* goes as far as painting can go in portraying character in repose, the *Battle of the Standard* shows Leonardo's equal power in portraying physical effort and struggle.

Da Vinci's foremost work, which is almost universally regarded as the greatest single achievement in painting in the world, is *The Last Supper.* Matched with this monumental triumph, other pictures of scriptural scenes fade into comparative insignificance. The crucifixions, transfigurations, Raphael's heading the list, in the Vatican, Titian's *Assumption* and all the Assumptions by all the other great artists, even the Sistine frescoes, taken separately, do not approach this masterpiece of Leonardo's, who spent ten years in painting it, and then left it unfinished. It is recorded that the monks, becoming tired of seeing the artist work, or apparently neglecting his work, complained bitterly of the delay. At times he would paint the whole day without stopping long enough to eat or drink, at other times he would stand for hours with folded arms before the picture, looking,

The Last Supper

By Leonardo da Vinci

Milan

studying, but never touching it at all. At times he would suddenly leave off modeling his Equestrian statue, hurry through the heat of the Italian summer sun to the refectory of the convent, add a few touches to *The Last Supper* and return as hurriedly and as unceremoniously as he had gone. Time has been scarcely less unkind to *The Last Supper* than to other works of Leonardo. It is now to most people nothing more than a magnificent ruin.

From every standpoint Leonardo's *Last Supper* meets every requirement of a perfect work of art. Plot, characterization, setting, plan, color, so far as we can judge, are all perfect, or were perfect. Giotto, the first who learned to tell a story in line and color, never dreamed of such refinement of plot as the picture discloses. With consummate art, Leonardo has divided the number of characters into four groups of three each, every attitude and every motion of each character being made a contributing factor to heighten the plot. The first group, composed of the three leading disciples, John, Judas and Peter, is placed upon the Master's right. John, whose face is very much like that of Christ, though less majestic, is seated next to him. Peter, leaning over towards John and clutching him by the shoulder, impetuously demands that John ask Christ who the traitor is. This inquiry is stamped as plainly upon Peter's face as pencil or brush can do it. Judas, sitting between John and Peter, grips the money bag securely and in his excitement upsets a salt-cellar with his arm. On his face is a look of anxious questioning. The group immediately on the Master's left is made up of James the Greater, Thomas and Philip. The expression on James's face is one of terror and amazement. Thomas, one of the most noticeable figures, holds his finger up to his forehead, saying in effect that he welcomes investigation. Philip, a handsome young man with smooth face, starts up and bends over toward James, at the

same time pointing towards his heart as if declaring his innocence of any knowledge of his Lord's betrayal. His face
has the worried look of one who fears that he may be
adjudged guilty. The two end groups are composed, the one
to the right of the Master, of Andrew, James the Less and
Bartholomew, and the other on his left of Matthew, Thaddeus and Simon, the latter directly facing Bartholomew at
the other end. / One of the most characteristic attitudes is
that of Andrew, an old man, who, drawing back horrified
and holding both hands up in front of his face, seems to
epitomize the awful tragedy about to be enacted. We appreciate more fully the genius of the artist when we compare
characters like Andrew and James the Greater, in whom
there is a similarity of age and motive and who are nevertheless so thoroughly individual, both terrified when they con-
front the tragic outcome of the Master's betrayal into the
hands of his enemies. James the Less is worried and lays
his hand on Peter's shoulder. Bartholomew, standing and
leaning forward with lips compressed, awaits eagerly John's
reply to the Master's words:

> "Verily, verily, I say unto you, that one of
> you shall betray me!"

The end group to the left is no less striking than the others.
Matthew, who is standing and pointing toward Christ, seems
to be saying, "Do you hear what is going on?" at the same
time looking at the two old men at the end. Thaddeus contracts his brows and seems about to strike his hands together,
the one resting on the table, the other raised. Simon seated
with his flowing robes looks at Thaddeus with an I-told-you-
so air, indicating by the motion of his hands and by his
countenance the grave nature of the situation. Thus in an
extremely blundering and inadequate way I have tried to
describe the details of, in many respects, the most wonderful

picture ever painted; it may give some conception, however, poor as it is, of the marvelous way in which Leonardo has told his story.

No less wonderful is the power of characterization which the picture discloses. Every one of these faces is a study, particularly those of Peter, Judas, and Christ. Leonardo's Christ is to me, at least, infinitely the best that ever has been drawn. The setting is perfect, the unity of it all superb, the color, before time and the fate of circumstance obliterated it, was, we may well believe, equal to the best. All in all, Leonardo's *Last Supper* ranks with the *Othello* and *Lear* of Shakspere and the *Oedipus Rex* of Sophocles as one of the greatest tragedies that the mind of man has ever conceived. As Michael Angelo's Sistine ceiling is the greatest epic, and Raphael's *Sistine Madonna,* painted to be carried as a banner in procession, the greatest hymn, and Correggio's lyrics of the brush the most transcendently beautiful and sweetest love lyrics in plastic art, so Leonardo's *Last Supper* is the greatest tragedy ever painted. There have been almost countless representations of the Last Supper, but only two of the number are really great productions, Leonardo's and Andrea del Sarto's in the Convent of San Salva. Mrs. Jamison goes into ecstasies over a *Last Supper* by Raphael, which Raphael did not paint. Andrea del Castagno's at St. Apollonia in Florence, which probably hinted something to Leonardo, is the next greatest after del Sarto's. Then there is Titian's *Last Supper,* a subject to which Titian could not do justice. Holbein at Basle has one with an especially hideous Judas, to whom physiognomists refer as a fine example of avarice and cruelty. There are many others, but in the last analysis there is only one *Last Supper,* as there is only one Shakspere or one Homer, and that is Leonardo's.

We come now to *Mona Lisa,* the most insoluble of Leonardo's pictures. It is not strictly speaking the greatest portrait in the world, for the reason that it is more than a portrait. Titian was the most brilliant portrait painter that ever lived, because he painted just enough of the ideal in his picture to make it a portrait and not a photograph; in other words, he paints the individual not the universal. Titian's portrait of the Duke of Urbino, for instance, is an idealized, but none the less, so far as we know, a correct picture of this particular Duke, who could, by no means, be made to pass for any duke whatsoever or for dukedom in general; he painted Francesco Rovere, Duke of Urbino only. But in the *Mona Lisa* who thinks of the daughter of Antonio Gherardini, or the third wife of del Gioconde? Does any one imagine that her face was ever the face of any one woman? What it stands for, what it strives to convey, no mortal knows, but it is safe to say that it is the ultimate contribution of the most daring genius of art to the greatest problem the world has ever known—the problem of personality. Goethe was perhaps more nearly correct than he thought when he declared that the profoundest truths of life are feminine rather than masculine. Shakspere's most subtle, most intricate and most perplexing character is not Hamlet or Iago but Cleopatra. Hamlet is a mirror of clearness compared with her. Raphael, who had a truer and broader view of humanity than any other man that ever lived, except Shakspere, painted women almost exclusively. The madonna face, the problem of motherhood was the secret of power with him. Botticelli's mysteries, as we shall see in another place, were locked up in the faces of women. Woman, a toy to Titian, a flash of light to Correggio, a divine inspiration to Raphael, an embodied idea to Botticelli, is to Leonardo a sphinx who holds fast locked within her fathomless glance the riddle of the universe. Leonardo's woman embodies the whole spirit of the Renaissance at the highest level it ever reached. To appreciate this, place the *Mona Lisa* beside the Venus of Milo, or any Greek ideals of womanhood and observe the infinite difference. On what does Venus meditate? On the fairness of life? of the joys of love? of her own superb physical charms? But of what does *Mona Lisa* think? Raphael's Madonnas, particularly the Sistine and the Granduca, are filled with the beauty of thought and the new born soul which was the gift of Christianity to womanhood, and Botticelli, through the wan faces of his Virgins and his Venuses, teaches a similar lesson; but Leonardo's conception is bolder, more daring, more profound. The most striking thing in the face of *Mona Lisa* is the sense of almost infinite power which it conveys. It is not a masculine power, but a power which seems to go back of both masculine and feminine to the primordial heart of things, to the abysmal chaos where Goethe's Mutter reigns supreme. Serene, undisturbed, triumphant, she stands as a type of the eternal feminine and locks within her bosom the secrets which the world can never know. It is thoroughly in harmony with this idea that she should be placed beside the sea, with stern cliffs of rock as a background. Well may Walter Pater say of her:

"The presence that rose thus so strangely beside the waters, is expressive of what in the ways of a thousand years men had come to desire. Hers is the head upon which all 'the ends of the world are come,' and the eyelids are a little weary. It is a beauty wrought out from within upon the flesh, the deposit, little cell by cell, of strange thoughts and fantastic reveries and exquisite passions. Set it for a moment beside one of those white Greek goddesses or beautiful women of antiquity, and how would they be troubled by this beauty, into which the soul with all its maladies has passed! All the thoughts and experience of the world have etched and moulded there, in that which they have of power to refine and make expressive the outward form, the animalism of Greece, the lust of Rome, the mysticism of the middle age with its spiritual ambition and imaginative loves, the return of the Pagan world, the sins of the Borgias. She is older than the rocks among which she sits; like the vampire, she has been dead many times, and learned the secrets of the grave; and has been a diver in deep seas, and keeps their fallen day about her; and trafficked for strange webs with Eastern merchants, and, as Leda, was the mother of Helen of Troy, and, as Saint Anne, the mother of Mary; and all this has been to her but as the sound of lyres and flutes, and lives only in the delicacy with which it has moulded the changing lineaments, and tinged the eyelids and the hands. The fancy of a perpetual life, sweeping together ten thousand experiences, is an old one; and modern philosophy has conceived the idea of humanity as wrought upon by, and summing up in itself, all modes of thought and life. Certainly Lady Lisa might stand as the embodiment of the old fancy, the symbol of the modern idea."

The greatest mystery of this mysterious woman is her smile. Vasari said of it in his quaint way that it was "so sweet while looking at it, one thinks it rather divine than human, and that it has ever been esteemed a wonderful work since life itself could exhibit no other appearance." Psychologists have tried to account for the origin of laughter and the smile, but Leonardo has put into the physical expression of *Mona Lisa* a meaning deeper than they have yet discovered. To him the smile is an evidence of power, calm, serene, undisturbed, self conscious.

In the following passages, taken from the section devoted to *Mona Lisa* in Merejkowski's powerful novel, *Leonardo da Vinci,* (by courtesy of G. P. Putnam's Sons, Publishers, New York and London), the writer speaks of

Gioconde's charms, of Leonardo's spiritual struggles and of the artist's power to blend the finite with infinity:

"There were moments when Leonardo rejoiced in her ethereal charm, which seemed above common humanity, yet was more real to him than aught belonging to everyday life. There were other moments in which he actually felt the beauty of the living woman.

"Leonardo found in her what is most rare, especially among women, instinctive wisdom. Sometimes by a chance sentence she would reveal herself so near, so akin to him in spirit, that he felt her his one and eternal friend, the sister of his soul. At these moments he would fain have overpassed the magic circle which divides contemplation from life. Was this love which united them? Alien to his nature was the passion which most men call love. Just as he ate no meat, because it seemed to him repulsive, so he refrained from women, because all material possession seemed to him coarse.

.   .   .   .

"At times he fancied he was subjecting her to a slow and terrible death. Her submissiveness alarmed him; it seemed limitless, like his own eternal search for knowledge, the delicate yet penetrating scrutiny to which he subjected her. Sooner or later he would have to decide what she was to him, a woman or a spirit. Past and Future had alike vanished from his memory; time had come to a standstill; it seemed as if she had always sat, and would ever thus sit before him, with that calm strange smile, and eyes like pure and fathomless water, the very counterpart of his own—two mirrors, each reflecting and absorbing the other into infinity. What he could not do in life he did by imagination; he blended the two images in one—mingled the reality and its reflection—the living woman and the immortal."

Doubtless this imaginative picture of the spiritual processes of the artist in the creation of the *Mona Lisa* is true. To paint "the things that lie beyond mortality" there must come to the artist moments when time and space, as sense perceptions, do not exist, when "there is no more near nor far," when "to the spirit's absoluteness all are like." It was during such moments, I doubt not, that Leonardo visualized the power back of and uniting both masculine and feminine and with unerring touch hid the mystery in Giaconde's fathomless eyes and in her inscrutable smile. Has she not heard the blasphemies of man, his insane boastings of superior wisdom, his beating of intellectual tom-toms and seen his sins and caprices and follies, conscious of her own deeper and farther searchings into the heart of things? To be able thus to look into the fathomless depths of personality and to smile and be serene at the stupidity and wickedness one sees there, is to possess superior power; and the mysterious smile upon the face of Mona Lisa is evidence of such a power.

Leonardo's people are all strong, superior beings; there is none of the pathos or weakness of del Sarto's creations, none of the wistfulness of Botticelli's, none of the sheer ponderousness of Angelo's; his was evidently a calm, serene genius which was master of itself, rising superior to the whirlwinds of passion and to the ordinary feelings of men. This thought is embodied in Merejkowski's book, especially in his chapter on Mona Lisa Gioconde, from which I quote once more:

"What more perfect union with the beloved could he have wished than in this secret and mystic intercourse, in the creation of this immortal image, this new being, born of them both, as a child of its parents, in which he and she were one? Nevertheless he felt that even in this mystic union, stainless as it was, there was danger—it might be greater danger than in the bond of ordinary fleshly love. They walked on the verge of a precipice where none had walked before, resisting the vertigo and the fatal attraction of the abyss. Between them were simple words, vague and uncompleted phrases, through which their secret showed as the sun shines through the morning mist. At times he thought what if the mist should scatter, and the blinding sun shine out which kills mystery, dissolves all phantoms? What if he or she should overstep the magic circle, materialize imagination into fact, contemplation into life? Had he a right to test a human soul, the soul of his life-long friend, his spiritual sister, as he tested the laws of mechanics, the structure of plants, the action of poison?"

It was out of such sovereignty, such mastery over passion and the flesh, that the austere, noble and immortal beauty of Leonardo's work was born. We may liken Raphael to Shakspere and Angelo to Milton or Dante, but there is no genius in any field of human achievement with which we may, with a sense of satisfying judgment, compare Leonardo. Perhaps the nearest parallel is Goethe. In his manifold knowledge, the vast range of his powers, his carefulness in details, the length of time he spent upon his master works, Leonardo in a measure resembles the great German poet. But Goethe was less profound, less daring and penetrating than Leonardo whose easy command of his resources and his own superb consciousness of power give him a unique place among the master minds of the world. There is a beauty, a mystery, about *Mona Lisa* and a depth of feeling in the Christ face in *The Last Supper* which appeal to us all more than the sublime unintelligibilities of *Faust*.

Leonardo is best appreciated perhaps to-day by a study of his numerous excellent sketches, which to a student, at least, are exceptionally interesting. Nearly all of them show that consciousness of superior power so prominent in all of his creations. Some are of grotesque monsters and unheard of creatures of fancy, some of strange, uncouth, gnarled

and twisted specimens of humanity. Most of them, however, are heads of women, and these, too, wear a smile.
There is one sketch which is peculiarly fascinating, that of
an old creature, like a satyr, with a hideously distorted nose,
and a beautiful girl, who looks at him contemptuously, perhaps a little curiously, but absolutely without a touch of
fear. The sensation in this sketch, as in all the others, is
that of power. Self-control, strength, determination, will,
these things are painted in every line. The man Leonardo,
flute player, courtier, mechanic, scientist, poet, artist, towers
above his fellow-men, a giant.

There is much more to record of Leonardo and little
space left to record it. He was the first to rediscover the
laws relating to the use of the lever, lost since the time of
Archimedes. He is usually regarded as the father of the
science of hydraulics. He was the first to promulgate the
theory of the molecular origin of water. He was likewise
the first to use the plus and minus signs in mathematics, and
in photography was the inventor of the camera obscura. He
actually made a sketch of a steam cannon, and in a note to
this sketch declared that with the help of steam a boat could
be set in motion, anticipating Robert Fulton, at least in the
idea, by three centuries. He planned a canal for the valley
of the Arno, which several centuries later was dug. There
was no field of industry or human knowledge to which he
did not contribute or into which he did not delve. His hand
could not fashion or make all that his too active mind conceived or complete all the splendid works he planned. To his
own people he was the "Wizard," and the schemes he formu-
lated and the problems he proposed we cannot even now, with
all the progress since his time, carry out or solve. The more
we know and study about Leonardo the more we are convinced that his intellect reached farther and struck out more
boldly and less unafraid than any of his age or since, per-

Beatrice D'Este　　　　　　　　　　　　　　　　　　　*Milan*

By Leonardo da Vinci

haps, into that inscrutable shadowy sea which the agnostics
of the nineteenth century called the Unknowable.   To most
intellects there is something terrifying in such far-flung
adventures. To Leonardo, more truly than to Newton, should
be applied Wordsworth's famous verse "a mind forever voy-
aging through strange seas of Thought, alone."   He steered
his adventurous craft into strange and unexplored seas of
thought and brought back mysteries which even to-day are
not fully understood.   To him, as to all who plunge into the
shadows, there was no doubt much that was unknown, but
nothing that was unknowable.   Who shall say to a genius
like his, or even to the ordinary intellect of man, "thus far
shalt thou go and no farther"?

Time has not dealt kindly with Leonardo.   It seems as
though nature, resentful of his persistent intrusion into her
secrets, has striven to delete all record of the knowledge he
acquired.   His greatest works, where not completely
destroyed, are in ruins, and even *Mona Lisa* smiles through
pigments almost colorless with age.   Withal, however, he
holds his place now, as at first, the immortality of genuine
fame being assured to him as long as man's consciousness
endures.

He left no family. Born homeless, he lived a star among
lesser stars and vanished like a meteor, leaving a heritage of
glory on the earth.   He wrought his magic in the world and
disappeared, leaving his papers to his favorite student and
his property, except some bequests to his servants, to his
brothers.   There was no Lucrezia in his life, as in the career
of del Sarto, and despite his experience as a courtier no
romance has ever been accredited to him, as there has been
to Raphael and to Botticelli.   He was a philosopher not in
writing systems of metaphysics, but in conquering life.   The
following lines are taken from one of his sonnets:

"Our joy and grief consist alike in this,
In knowing what to will and what to do,
But only he whose judgment never strays
Beyond the threshold of the right, learns this."

A thought singularly parallel to the lines of the old English dramatist, George Chapman:

"There is no danger to the man who knows
What life and death is; there's not any law
Exceeds his knowledge; neither is it lawful
That he should stoop to any other law."

Each of these excerpts contain as much philosophy as any four lines ever written. These words of Leonardo and Chapman reveal the secret of the artist's power which made him the favorite of every prince, and the talisman of the poet which enabled him to win, over even the redoubtable Shakspere, the favor of his sovereign. In closing we inquire if Leonardo always triumphed and *Mona Lisa* always smiled. Let his own words answer:

"Nor is it always good to have one's wish;
What seemeth sweet full oft to bitter turns,
Fulfilled desire hath made mine eyes to weep!"

Back of the smile, far away in the fathomless eyes of *Mona Lisa,* there must, there does, spring life's fountain of tears.

BOTTICELLI

* * * * * *

Painter of the Ideal

Portrait of Botticelli   *Florence*

BOTTICELLI

On a day in May of the year 1490 a man, apparently lost in deep meditation, entered the Duomo in Florence where Savonarola was hurling his terrible denunciations against sins and sinners.

"Beware!" cried the great preacher, "behold the Lord mighty to avenge cometh to execute judgment upon you and yours. And ye who through brush and chisel have helped to turn men's minds from the living Jehovah, peace, the blessed peace of God which stills the restless sorrow of the heart shall be yours neither in this world nor in that which is to come."

The man entered the cathedral just at the moment when these words burst from the throat of the speaker. His eye met the eye of Savonarola at its full potency of religious fervor, and the ardent priest seemed to communicate to the man some occult power or influence, for the latter turned and immediately left the cathedral. He hurried to his home, gathered all his finished and unfinished Venuses and Floras together and burned them. Fortunately, for the world of art the pictures destroyed were only those which were in his own house. Had he destroyed all of his paintings, in his obsession of religious frenzy, the world of art and beauty would have sustained an irreparable loss, and the work of Botticelli would never have filled the earth with his fame, nor the souls of men and women with glory. He was forty-three years old at this time and was looked upon as the best painter in Florence, but in that hour Botticelli's career as an artist ended. The peace he had vainly sought in his art had, as he believed, come to him in another way, but the work into

37

which he had put the story of his struggles and aspirations was to live forever; this was to constitute his greatness and to be his glory throughout all generations.

Alessandro dei Filipepi, surnamed Botticelli, a tanner's son, was born in Florence in 1447. Very little is known about his life. He was apprenticed when but a boy to a goldsmith named Botticelli, whose patronym he took and by his genius immortalized. It is recorded that the wealthy jeweler looked with compassion upon the poor apprentice, whose most insignificant and crudest work would some day be worth in actual money value more than all the possessions of the merchant. The goldsmith's calling in those days was one of art, and even to-day the work of the Florentine jeweler is an artistic one. Next to the galleries and cathedrals the jeweler's shops which line the Ponte Vecchio are most interesting to a lover and student of beauty. But Alessandro Filipepi Botticelli, the apprentice, was not destined to be a goldsmith, and after a few years he was transferred to the studio of that royal scalawag in the world of art, Fra Lippo Lippi.

One of the peculiarities of Botticelli's genius was his ability to assimilate so much of Lippi's method and to employ it in such a different way. No two artists were so essentially opposite as Sandro and Fra Lippo Lippi. The latter was a realist in the full sense of the word, a materialistic Falstaffian child of the world who never painted an angel that was not fat and overfed and with lips suggestive of the epicure. Botticelli was, on the contrary, the most extreme idealist in the history of painting. None of his creations even remotely suggest too much flesh, but are *spirituelle* creations of beauty and grace. Lippo Lippi's people all smile, Botticelli's are sad and wan. The glory of the flesh is the cardinal tenet of the Carmelite friar, while Sandro's wistful eyes look through their mortal casements as from prison windows whose earthly bars shut out the heaven's light they vainly seek to reach.

At the age of twenty, Botticelli left the tutelage of Fra Lippo and came under the influence of Verrochio. His first great picture, the famous *Madonna of the Louvre,* in which the Virgin Mother bends forward to kiss her child, was produced at this time. It seems almost incredible that the work considered by some authorities among his greatest was done at the age of twenty-two. It should be remembered, however, that many of the greatest things men have ever done have been accomplished at a very early age. Bryant wrote *Thanatopsis* at eighteen, Marlowe *Tamburlaine* at twenty, and Keats produced all of his superb body of poetry before twenty-seven, to say nothing of such composers as Mozart and others. In the *Madonna of the Louvre* the wan and sorrowful face of the Christ mother contains no note of joy; the sadness and the wistfulness of the Botticelli face are seen in this picture in the fulness of perfection. The Christ child is also sad with a yearning for human love in its innocent face that contrasts noticeably with the hopeless, unspoken sorrow of the mother. Botticelli is, at twenty-two, apparently disillusioned and realizes that life's promised joys are but hollow mockeries, shot through and through as they are with pain and sorrow, which even the best and wisest cannot escape.

At twenty-four the painter was working with the Pollajuoli brothers, two very skilful anatomists. While with them he painted *Fortitude* which Ruskin has so highly extolled, and which so much resembles many of the genuine Pollajuolis that Morelli and others have attributed it to them, an attribution which, I think, no one who appreciates or understands the significance of Botticelli's message in art will accept. It is true that the figure and the attitude of the woman are like Pollajuoli's, but the face is Botticelli's and

his alone. Worn and weary with the sorrows and the struggles she has endured, *Fortitude* awaits the call to other sorrows, other conflicts, other trials of endurance, with no
thought of giving up or yielding. Like the *Madonna of the
Louvre,* with the wistful, sorrowing eyes, she asks the unresponsive silence why such things as pain and sorrow, as
Gethsemanes and crowns of thorns and Calvarys must be;
why suffering and endurance are required in a world of
beauty where joy and gladness should reign instead of pain
and sorrow; not that she is unwilling or afraid to suffer, only
the irrepressible "why" is on her lips, while in every line of
her face an everlasting determination is written into an
"everlasting yea." The figure of *Fortitude,* whether by Botticelli or another, is not attractive, the countenance cannot be
called beautiful, as beauty is judged by the world, but there
is a light in the eyes, a glory in the face, which is a part of
the beauty that never fades, something more than mere
sensuous attraction. In both of these pictures, as in all of
Botticelli's, there is no note of rebellion, no denial of the
supreme value of the goal which is sought, but only the
plaintive wish that the same goal might be reached in a
different way, that the cup might pass, the Gethsemane be
shunned, the Calvary be avoided.

It was about this time that the skill of Sandro attracted
the attention of Lorenzo the Magnificent. From his youth
Botticelli had been attached to the noble family of the Vespucci, a family known to Americans through a descendant
of Lorenzo, Americus Vespucci, for whom America was
named. His connection with this family and his relations
with Lorenzo were the source of the most romantic incident
ever known in the life of an Italian painter. Simonetta
Vespucci was renowned for her beauty and charm far beyond
the bounds of Florence. She is thus described by Poliziano,
one of the best known writers of his time:

> "Among many excellent gifts she had the
> sweetest and most attractive manners, so that
> all those who enjoyed the privilege of her friend-
> ship, thought themselves beloved by her, and it
> seemed almost impossible that so many men could
> love her without exciting any jealousy, and so
> many women praise her without feeling any sense
> of envy."

She was betrothed to the handsome Giuliano de Medici, the
younger brother of Lorenzo, and the idol of the Florentine
people. That a poor artist, a tanner's son, should look with
a lover's eyes upon the daughter of a Medici was an unheard
of thing and a very grave offense. His love, of course, was
hopeless, the wretched lover scarcely daring to acknowledge
his passion to his own soul. But the fair Simonetta was not
destined to live long for either husband or lover. In a little
while she died of consumption, Giuliano surviving her but
a short time. All Florence mourned for the fair maiden and
princess, but none more deeply than the despairing artist.
The insoluble "why" which he painted on every wistful face
that looks out from his canvases was on his lips. Why did
the young, the fair, the good have to die? The spoken and
unspoken question of Hamlet, "How can such things be?"
was ever in his brain. This question is asked in all of his
paintings from this time on. Every wistful Madonna, every
Venus, every Flora of the woods has it written in her eyes
and on her face. After this Sandro could not have distilled
very much pleasure from life, though his work continued to
grow better and better. Lorenzo invited him to his home and
with frank magnanimity treated him as one of his own family. In the palace of the Medici he met Poliziano and others
of the most brilliant Humanists and philosophers of the
Renaissance, to whose learned discourses on the Greek and
Latin philosophy and literature he listened in the cloistered
alcoves of the New Academy. Fortune smiled upon him and

he became famous, but wistful faces still looked out of his canvases and the note of sadness was still there.

The record of Botticelli's life after this event, like that of Shakspere's, is but the story of his work. With but one exception, and that late in life, none of his paintings was signed. At twenty-nine he is known to have been painting in the Campo Santo at Pisa. Returning to Florence he began the series of *Tondi* or round paintings which have become so famous. These pictures are scattered all over the world, but the most beautiful of them, the *Madonna della Melagrana* and the *Madonna of the Magnificat,* are in the third Tuscan room of the Uffizi Gallery in Florence. No one who has ever seen these powerful paintings with the weird, sad eyes looking at you after four hundred years of imprisonment can ever forget them. They are the most striking pictures, all things considered, in the gallery.

In 1478, after the Pozzi conspiracy, Florence became embroiled in a war with the Pope and his ally, Fernante, the powerful King of Naples. For a while it looked as if the city would be taken by the enemy, a doom which was averted by the diplomacy of Lorenzo who went alone as his own ambassador to Naples. Lorenzo appealed so strongly to the generosity of Fernante, whose savage disposition was proverbial throughout Italy, that he won the Neapolitan king and secured his friendship for his people. Amid the general rejoicing over this victory Botticelli seems for the moment to have forgotten the burden of sorrow which usually overshadowed his soul and painted the *Pallas and the Centaur,* Pallas representing Lorenzo and the Centaur the half-savage Fernante. This was the last picture of Botticelli to be discovered (1894), and now hangs in the throne room of the royal apartments of the Pitti palace. It is considered one of the greatest treasures of the King of Italy, and has a place of distinction accorded no other picture in Florence.

Pallas and the Centaur　　　　　　　　　　　　　　　*Florence*

By Botticelli

The tone of sadness is absent here, though the expression of Pallas can hardly be called joyous.

About the same time, probably in 1476, he painted the *Adoration of the Magi* in which he represents nearly all the prominent people of his day under the guise of Wise Men and their attendants. The first Magi represents Cosimo de Medici and the second and third his two sons. The artist painted his own portrait in this picture—one of the choice treasures of the Uffizi Gallery. The dates of his great mythological pictures, the *Primavera* and the *Birth of Venus,* are uncertain but probably later than 1481, when he was summoned to Rome by Pope Sixtus IV. to paint in the Sistine Chapel.

The three frescoes, representing scenes from the life of Moses, are interesting as specimens of Botticelli's artistic power; his name, however, if it had to depend upon these alone, would not be immortal. A student of Sandro finds much in them to admire, while others pass them by forgetting their existence in the presence of the overshadowing glory of Angelo. It seems that the unfettered genius of the artist was not at home in the splendid chapel of the Vatican and that his capricious fancy could pour out its full treasures only when it was free from all external restrictions. The three frescoes represent *The Punishment of Korah, Episodes in the Life of Moses,* and the *Purification of the Leper.* The last named picture, painted exactly opposite the papal throne, also contains scenes from the Temptation of Christ, in which the painter indulged in a freak of independence whose daring illustrates the rebellious spirit in which the work seems to have been done. Pope Sixtus belonged to the Franciscan order which Botticelli disregarded by attiring the Devil in the *Temptation* in robes of a Franciscan monk, the pontiff when seated on his throne being compelled to look at the enemy of mankind clad in the habiliments of his own order.

The picture of Moses with the daughters of Jethro is to me the most beautiful of the three. There is a charm in the rural scenery, in the water, in the shade cast by the trees, suggestive of an idyl of Theocritus or Spenser or one from the plays of Fletcher or Jonson.

After completing these frescoes for Sixtus, Botticelli returned to Florence. His next three pictures—the *Madonna of the Magnificat,* the *Primavera,* and the *Birth of Venus*— represent the climax of his genius. His technique in these paintings reached its highest perfection, and his mastery of linear motion and his delicacy of shading and tint are here seen at their best. He seems to have painted his whole soul in these pictures and through them sought to tell to the uttermost the message which the World-Spirit had entrusted to him.

He also did a frescoe of *St. Augustine* in the church of the Ognissanti. Vasari, referring to this powerful work, says that the artist "put forth his greatest powers to surpass all his contemporaries, especially Domenico Ghirlandajo, who had painted a *St. Jerome* on the opposite wall. Sparing no pains he thus produced a work of extraordinary merit." Vasari, with his courtier-like disposition, which saw no motive higher or stronger than a jealous rivalry for fame, never quite appreciated the genius or the exquisitely attuned nature of Botticelli, and could not understand the real reason for the unsparing pains of the artist. Had rivalry of Ghirlandajo been his motive the Sistine Chapel, the greatest building for artistic work in the world, would have been a more auspicious field of contest. Ghirlandajo, Perugino and Rosselli were his rivals there, and yet Botticelli seemed absolutely indifferent as to his achievements, if not indeed resentful that he had been called away from his work in Florence for what seemed to be a greater work; while in the little

church of the Ognissanti, one of the least known of all the
shrines in the city, he takes infinite pains, working with all
his energies, sparing neither time nor labor, to produce a
masterpiece. There was a deeper reason for this than Vasari
discerned. Simonetta Vespucci was buried in this church
and Botticelli was painting his *St. Augustine* on the wall of
the Vespucci Chapel in which the body of his beloved reposed.
It requires but little stretching of the imagination to picture
Sandro, the idealist, working under the inspiration of her
presence by day and in the thought of her spirit brooding
over the fresco by night, approving or disapproving as he
was skilful or unskilful in his work. The *St. Augustine* is
unquestionably a masterpiece. The scholar saint sits, unmi-
tred, with his mantle falling in majestic folds about him.
Alone, with one hand clasped above his breast, the other
holding a book which his eyes do not see, he looks into
infinity with an expression of questioning, the whole picture
telling a story which is supremely impressive. The "why"
that is painted in every face and speaks in every eye of every
picture which he painted after the death of Simonetta Vespucci is unusually noticeable in the *St. Augustine.* The
Madonna of the Magnificat and the *Madonna of the Melagrana* are sad because the mother of the Son of God must
suffer so terribly that she may be worthy of her supreme
exaltation; the *Venus* of the Uffizi is sad because she realizes
that there must remain for her the bitter dregs of satiety in
every cup she drains; in *St. Augustine,* the philosopher pon-
ders over the inexplicable problems of the intellect which
he cannot solve but which nevertheless press upon him constantly for solution, returning again and again like an evil
spirit to torment him. Botticelli has drawn no more impressive figure, and the world may be challenged to produce a
fresco which better tells the story which the artist wanted to
proclaim. No other picture tells quite so much of the intel-

lect baffled, or is such an incarnation of the unsatisfied spirit of knowledge.

Sandro painted one more great picture before his career was practically ended by Savonarola's preaching. This picture, which now hangs in the small room next to the famous Tribuna, is the most poignant of all he ever painted and the one in which he seems to have thrown all the energies of his being—if he could go farther than in the *Magnificat,* the *Primavera,* or the *Birth of Venus.* As he had previously pictured the Inexplicable in religion, the Inexplicable in love, and the Inexplicable in philosophy, he now pictures the Inexplicable in justice. *Calumny* is the name of this painting, the subject of which was taken from Lucian's description of a lost picture by Apelles, the foremost painter of ancient Greece. *Calumny* represents a man with long ears seated upon a throne of justice with two women, Ignorance and Suspicion, one of whom stands on either side of his chair. Immediately before him stands Calumny, a very beautiful woman with an exceptionally subtle face. In her left hand she holds a flaming torch, while with her right she hales by the hair a young man who lifts his hands as if praying. She is attended by two women, Hypocrisy and Deceit, who bedeck her with ornaments. Beyond this group of which Calumny is the central figure stands Remorse, a hideous female form, clad in sordid garments of tattered rags. Near her is Truth, undraped, modest, and embarrassed. *Calumny* is a small picture and hangs with Leonardo's *Medusa* in the same room of the Uffizi Gallery. There is a fierce energy about this production which accentuates its interest, though it mars its artistic value. With intense hatred he has portrayed the vain and triumphant Calumny and with no less commiseration the helpless innocence of her victim. Relentlessly, implacably, he pictures the misery of Remorse which comes too late, while with bitter irony he accentuates the weakness of the

The Calumny   By Botticelli   *Florence*

incompetent judge. It is a picture of the times and a prophecy of the avenging wrath of Savonarola. *Calumny* was Botticelli's last great picture, and calls to mind that bitter outburst of Shakspere's heart in which he portrays the Athenian Timon, the misanthropic exile living upon roots and water away from the follies and the crimes of men. After *Hamlet* and *Lear* Shakspere writes *Timon of Athens,* after the *Primavera* and the *Magnificat* Botticelli paints the *Calumny.* The times of Savonarola are now at hand.

Sandro's last picture, *The Nativity,* is the only one he signed. The painting seems to be a vision of Savonarola's triumph and the signature, which follows, an epitome of Savonarola's wrath:

"This picture, I, Alessandro, painted at the end of the year 1500, during the troubles of Italy in the half-time after the time which was prophesied in the Eleventh of St. John and the Second Woe of the Apocalypse, when the devil was loosed upon the earth for three and a half years. Afterwards he shall be put in chains according to the Twelfth, and we shall see him trodden under foot as in this picture."

It had been just three and a half years since he had seen the flames consume the body of Savonarola, and Botticelli tells us in his picture and in his written testimony that his faith in the Friar has never wavered, and that he is still looking forward to the time when the great reformer's teachings shall triumph over evil.

The Nativity, his most optimistic picture, was really Botticelli's farewell to pictorial art, as *The Tempest,* Shakspere's most optimistic play, was the poet's farewell to dramatic art. The remaining ten years of his life were spent in illustrating Dante and doing other things of comparatively little value. His last days were passed in poverty and seclusion. He had mingled all his life with his fellow artists, holding aloof from them, however, in manner and method. They had not understood him, and he had not cared. He has been abundantly rewarded since. Botticellis are now more valuable than diamonds, and but a little more than forty years since a set of his drawings was considered cheap at ten thousand dollars.

Botticelli died on May 17, 1510, and was buried in the church of the Ognissanti, on a day in May where a little less than forty years before the body of Simonetta Vespucci was inhumed. After all his restless and unsatisfied longing let us hope that he was at peace in the same sanctuary with her whom he loved and whom he immortalized in every sad, questioning, Madonna and Venus which look out from their canvases with large wistful eyes. His *St. Augustine* looks down tenderly upon both and gives them its benediction. The beams of the sun as it goes down in the west illuminate the gorgeous tints of the glorious colors of this fresco. At this hour all is still save the ripple of the Arno outside and the soft spirit-voice of Simonetta which the visitor at times imagines he hears speaking to her artist-lover, telling him he has done well. It was at this hour of the day when I last stood by the grave of Botticelli. The dying sun poured his glory full on the grave, questioning countenance of the scholar saint. The Arno rippled by Ognissanti's walls. The spirit of love seemed to brood over the place, and the following words of Browning, who went often to this cathedral when he lived in Florence, involuntarily came back to my memory:

"Is it too late then, Evelyn Hope?
What, your soul was pure and true,
The good stars met in your horoscope;
Made you of spirit, fire and dew—
And just because I (am) thrice as old
And our paths in the world diverged so wide,
Each was naught to each, must I be told?
We were fellow mortals, naught beside?"

Detail of the Crowning of the Virgin
By Botticelli

Florence

"No, indeed! for God above
Is great to grant, as mighty to make,
And creates the love to reward the love;
I claim you, still for my own love's sake!
Delayed it may be for more lives yet,
Through worlds I shall traverse, not a few:
Much is to learn, much to forget
Ere the time be come for taking you."

The paintings of Botticelli may be classified as religious, classical, and allegorical. More than eighty of his pictures have been preserved, though widely scattered, the best among them, however, being still in Italy. The greatest of his religious pictures, aside from the frescoes already mentioned, are the *Madonna of the Louvre,* the *Madonna Melagrana,* the *Magnificat,* the *Judith,* and the *Adoration of the Magi* in the Uffizi, *The Coronation of the Virgin* in the Academy, *The Nativity* in the National Gallery and *The Entombment* in the Museum Poldi-Pezzoli, Milan.

The Entombment is a great picture. It has as much feeling as Giotto's at Padua, but scarcely as much delicacy as Fra Bartolommeo's masterpiece in Florence. Its most impressive touch is Joseph holding up a crown of thorns in his right hand with an expression of questioning which says more plainly than words: "Why was it necessary for Him to wear this?" *The Coronation of the Virgin* in the Academy at Florence is one of Botticelli's best character studies. The upper part of the picture is quite conventional, but the lower part, which includes the pictures of four saints, reveals a master's hand. The *Judith* in the Uffizi is a small painting containing all the characteristics of Botticelli's work. It is a very different production from Allori's in the Pitti, which represents a proud, triumphant girl who thinks only of the victory she has won and nothing of the murder of the tyrant by which it was achieved. It is different from Botticelli's Judith, who, while conscious of triumph, is also sad because to secure the victory her hands must perforce be stained with blood. As Brutus, who slew Caesar to maintain Rome's liberties, could never quite wash clean the stain from his hands, so Judith never feels quite free from the blood-guiltiness of the murder of Holofernes, despite the fact that it was the only way by which her country's freedom could be achieved. Mention has already been made of *The Nativity* in the National Gallery. It is a small picture, crowded with figures and interesting above others because it is his last and has his signature and inscription in Greek. The centre shows the manger with the infant Jesus and the mother kneeling before the child in adoration, while heavenly hosts sing paeans of joy. The three figures in the Dominican habit at the lower part of the picture are supposed to represent Savonarola and the two monks who were burned with him; three angels clasp them ready to bear them to heaven. This picture seems to say that its creator's restless spirit had found peace and that the problem of pain and sorrow was no longer insoluble. As the *Calumny* bears some analogy to *Timon of Athens* and Shakspere's misanthropy, so *The Nativity* resembles *The Tempest* in its serenity. The two great *tondi,* the *Madonna of the Pomegranate,* or *Melagrana,* as it is sometimes called, and the *Madonna of the Magnificat,* are Botticelli's greatest Madonnas, and in many respects his greatest pictures. Their wondrous fascination never grows less. The *Melagrana* is more expressive, the *Magnificat* is richer. To see these two paintings is alone worth a trip to Florence.

Botticelli's fame, however, rests more upon his classical pictures than upon his Madonnas. The prevailing Renaissance spirit is better expressed in these than in the others, and the subjects were more in harmony with his own moods than in altar pieces, too frequently made to order. Three of these classical pictures, out of nearly a dozen, have become household words in the realm of painting—the *Primavera,* or

Judith   *Florence*

By Botticelli

Spring, in the Academy at Florence, the *Birth of Venus* in the Uffizi Gallery and the *Mars and Venus* in the National Gallery in London.

Some critics, and some others, do not like Botticelli's classical pictures, but they are a diminishing tribe. It is a fact, patent to every one who visits the Uffizi, that the Venus room is always crowded. Both the *Birth of Venus* and the *Primavera* are thoroughly typical of their creator. The *Primavera* is supposed to have been inspired by Simonetta, as it contains idealized portraits of both her and Giuliano de Medici. It is Botticelli's largest and most widely discussed picture. Its setting is superb with its background of forest, with its harmony of movement and with its wealth of color and design. The painting is indeed allegorical, but we assign it to the classical group because the allegorical features are less prominent than the mythological. The central figures in the picture are Venus and Spring, the former directly in the centre, the latter a little in the front and to the left of Venus. On the right of the goddess are the three Graces, lightly draped, and revealing a superb mastery of exquisite linear motion. No picture in the world portrays the Graces so truly and exquisitely graceful as this. Hermes, in the likeness of Giuliano de Medici, on her extreme right, dispels with his magic wand the unwholesome mists which still linger among the leaves of the orange trees. Simonetta herself as the Goddess of Spring, supremely conscious of her charms, comes tripping proudly through the forest shaking the roses from her garments, her hair wreathed with blue cornflowers and daisies, her white robe itself a pattern of flowers of every hue, trailing fresh ivy and briar rose, while Flora, flying from the embrace of Zephyr, drops rose-buds and anemones from her lips.

Of the two principal characters in the *Primavera,* Venus and Spring, the former, though worthy of extended study,

must be dismissed with a word.   She is more unlike the real
goddess than any Venus ever painted, chiseled or sung.   There
seems to have been a deeply concealed malice in the painter
in representing her as he did, something like that of his clothing the Devil in the Franciscan habit in his Sistine fresco.
He makes Venus feel the responsibilities of life and not
merely revel in the enjoyments of the gay and joyous side
of her nature.   But Spring, who is after all the protagonist
in this picture drama, is the most perplexing.   Tradition says
that she is an idealized Simonetta Vespucci, but there is
something about her which repels rather than attracts and
we can scarcely think a lover would thus idealize his goddess.
There are few faces more austerely pitiless or more proudly
unfeeling than hers.   She is a queen, a merciless one, and to
be commiserated is the victim who cannot escape her power.
Even the flowers in her hair give her a sort of serpentine
charm which ensnares like magic amulets with its irresistible
might.   Her eyes are coldly curious, akin somewhat to those
of a scientific vivisectionist who measures carelessly the
amount of suffering his victim can stand.   One shudders at
the thin locks which fall over her face, as if each hair had
the drawing strength of a thousand cables, were she to release
her uncanny energies.

Was this really the Simonetta of whom Poliziano wrote
his sugared verses and for whom all Florence mourned?   No,
it was not she; but it was the Simonetta that Botticelli sometimes saw in his dreams when the bitter agony of his life
pressed heavily upon him; it was the Simonetta that he saw
in those moments when he asked himself why things must
be as they are, why love, the richest and the best thing in the
consciousness of the race, must carry with it such a sting,
why every joy involves a greater sorrow?

The other two classical pictures, the *Birth of Venus* and
Venus and Mars, are both idealizations of the Christian

The Spring   By Botticelli   Florence

Paganism or the Pagan Christianity of the Renaissance. Venus is no longer the beautiful soulless woman of Phidias or Praxiteles, but rather the incarnation of a Passion whose greater responsibility has just dawned upon her mind. She is born into another and a higher world, a world of infinite care and anxiety and sorrow; and yet confronting all this she is still Venus, though a much perplexed Venus. No Venus of Phidias or Apelles would long to be clad, as Botticelli's does, not because of any desire for raiment, but because her new environment requires it. In the *Mars and Venus* in the National Gallery another side of the Renaissance spirit is revealed. There is an expression of infinite affection on her face as she watches over her sleeping lover; there is also an expression which reveals a feeling of uncertainty as to whether this attitude of anxious love is not too serious for her. Botticelli's Venus is a compromise between Titian's and Raphael's, if such a comparison is permissible. Titian's Venus is the old Greek ideal of purely sensual attractiveness, a little more beautiful than the Greek, if anything, because in spite of himself Titian endowed her with the semblance of a soul, while Raphael's is the most sublime incarnation of motherhood, the glory of Judaism and Christianity, culminating in the worship of the Virgin almost to the exclusion of her Son. Botticelli tried to harmonize the two conceptions, an impossible task, and because it was impossible, he failed. Venus and Mary, Pagan love and Christian motherhood, are hard to reconcile, though the task before and since the time of Botticelli has been many times attempted.

We have noticed already the greatest of Sandro's strictly allegorical pictures, the *Pallas and the Centaur,* the *Fortitude,* and the *Calumny.* Besides his religious, classical and allegorical pictures Botticelli painted nine or ten portraits, the best of which are those of *Pietro de Medici* in the Uffizi Gallery and of *Simonetta Vespucci* in the Pitti. There is also another portrait of *Simonetta* in the Berlin Gallery and one of *Giuliano de Medici*.

Volumes might be written, as volumes have been written, about his work. In this study, however, there remains yet to be noticed only the significance of his message and the motives which inspired it.

Botticelli was emphatically an idealist in art, that is, he expressed as nearly as could be done on canvas those thoughts and ideas which the faces of his plaintive Venuses and Madonnas so unmistakably reveal, faces which are a revelation of the longings of his own soul for an ideal world, for a place of escape from the anxieties and sorrows of this present existence, for a mystical fountain of healing and peace. For this idealism of Botticelli three things, I think, were chiefly responsible: The first of these was the rise of Humanism and the effort to reconcile Pagan beliefs and Christianity; this was the dominant idea of his time and of which he was in painting the most distinguished exponent; the second was his own temperament, and the third his personal experience.

The problem of Humanism, the aim of which was to reconcile the natural religion of beauty and joy and culture, embodied in Greek art and philosophy, with the supernatural religion of sorrow and suffering and struggle, embodied in Christianity, was the question which dominated and perplexed the mind of every Renaissance scholar. It was the main tenet of Humanism that nothing that had ever interested men and women can wholly lose its power or its vitalizing force. This doctrine received tremendous momentum at the Council of Florence in 1459, fifteen years before Botticelli was born, which was called to deliberate upon the proposed union of the Greek and Latin churches. Upon this occasion prominent Greek scholars, particularly Gemistos Pletho, the learned leader of the Neo-Platonists of his time,

visited Florence, bringing with them a plan for reconciling
the teachings of the Platonic and Christian systems of
thought and religion. Pletho was induced by Cosimo de
Medici, over whom the former had a commanding influence,
to found a school of philosophy after the manner of the
ancient Academy at Athens. This New Academy, for such
it was named, soon became the resort of the most intellectual
and cultured men of the time. The fall of Constantinople
brought to Italy many more of the choicest spirits of modern
Greece.

Among those who attended the splendid banquets of
Lorenzo de Medici in the groves of the New Academy was
Massilio Ficino who, though a dignitary of the church, kept
a votive lamp continually burning before a bust of Plato.
There were also the half Greek and half Christian Agnolo
Poliziano, or Politian as he is usually called, the foremost
scholar of his day, the translator of Homer and Hippocrates
into Latin and, in a certain sense, the founder of modern
Italian poetry; and Pulci, author of one of the greatest of
Italian romantic poems, the *Morgante Maggiore,* a strange
medley of Christian faith and Pagan fancies, in which an
invocation to the Virgin Mary is followed almost immediately by a hymn to Venus. Another who attended these
famous banquets was that "phoenix of genius," as he was
called, the famous Mirandola, who knew Greek and Hebrew
lore as it has seldom, if ever, been known before or since,
and who after a vain attempt to reconcile the conflicting systems of Plato and Christ became at last, like Botticelli, a
disciple of Savonarola.

It was at the feet of these men that Botticelli sat and
listened and meditated, and then went forth to paint on his
immortal canvases the problems which neither he nor they
could solve. Being an artist to the core, he could most fully
appreciate the beauty of the Greek ideal, but being a devout

Christian, descended from Christian ancestors, he could not accept it as it was. To him who had once understood the dignity of a higher life the Greek ideal was inadequate and impossible; at the same time there was a beauty about its very completeness, about the physical charm of its Venus and its Apollo, which made the artist hesitate and think, and perhaps regret, when he confronted the visions of an inscrutable and boundless eternity to be achieved here and attained hereafter only through this higher life of unsatisfied longing with all of its pain and sorrow. This struggle in his own soul between the two ideals, the one of beauty and joy, the other of infinite, unsatisfied longing, is revealed in the faces of his Venuses and his Madonnas. In these insoluble problems of Humanism are to be found one motive for the character of Botticelli's work.

The second source of the painter's idealism is found, I think, in his temperament. His nature was one of delicate sensitiveness, of purely esthetic tastes, of love for the ideal and dislike of the actual. He was a dreamer, and the *spirituelle* faces of his Venuses and Madonnas are the embodiments of dreams which to him, as to every dreamer and idealist, were more real than the actual. We love them just because they are incarnations of the ideal.

His personal experience is the third motive and sufficiently accounts for many characteristics of his work. Whatever people may say about the universality of genius and the aloofness of the creator from his creation, the fact remains that the personal equation is a prominent factor, if not the most prominent, in creating any work of art. Shakspere's dramas, the critics to the contrary, are largely Shakspere's experiences at different periods of his life, without which his productions had been different from what they are. This is true of all creative artists, among whom Botticelli is no exception. That all of his wan, plaintive Madonnas and his

Madonna and Six Angels   *Florence*

By Botticelli

dissatisfied Venuses are an expression only of the Humanist philosophy, or of his own idealistic temperament entirely, I do not believe. It does not appear to be sound criticism to so interpret them. These are contributory motives. It is true that the story of his relations with Simonetta Vespucci is a matter of legend, perhaps as well, though no better, attested than most of the romances which have been recorded about the painters of his time. But unlike many of the others, Botticelli's history is written in his paintings and needs only a sympathetic appreciation to reveal it. With the blight of a hopeless love in his soul he wrote its story into every picture he painted. Other painters might exalt the Mother of Christ and picture her in the joy of the honor which was hers, but not so with Botticelli; the only Virgin his imagination could picture was the sorrowful woman who saw Gethsemane and Calvary ever before her eyes. Likewise, other artists might paint light-hearted Venuses with the ardor of passion upon the face and the joys of love in the heart, while he saw only the dark and cruel side of human affection. He did not condemn love because the crown of happiness could not be his, but he none the less felt most bitterly the anguish of its loss. That he nowhere appears jealous of her betrothed is a noble trait in his character. He has painted Giuliano de Medici several times and always sympathetically and fondly. He loved Simonetta as an ideal, as a dream, which he could never hope to possess, but its very hopelessness left a sting more poignant than death.

The concluding years of Botticelli's life were spent in the study of Dante. Doubtless the story of the Poet's love for Beatrice, similar to his own, found a response in his soul. He was acquainted also with the story of Petrarch and Laura de Sade. His idol, unlike these, had a real, tangible existence; he had known and had seen her day after day and had heard the music of her voice. She was too real to be an ideal only, and the sting of her loss was the more bitter on that account.   Hence, the everlasting "Why must it be so?" is asked in every face he painted.

MICHAEL ANGELO

. . . . . .

Painter of the Sublime

MICHAEL ANGELO

A visitor in Rome feels the invisible presence of two men—Julius Caesar and Michael Angelo—as he feels the presence of no others. Every relic of ancient Roman civilization recalls the mighty Julius, and no less does the Florentine giant overshadow his contemporaries. The history of Michael Angelo is an open book compared with that of Leonardo or Botticelli, and yet in spite of this it is extremely difficult to form a correct estimate of the man. He was a law unto himself, having no forerunners in the larger sense and leaving no descendants. He was never married and never felt, so far as any record goes, the slightest love, aside from a Platonic one, for any woman. His ideals of beauty were all masculine, and the few figures of women which he painted or chiseled have distinctly masculine traits. The word "girl" does not seem to have been in Michael's vocabulary. His Eve of the Sistine ceiling is a mature woman and his Night and Dawn in the chapel of San Lorenzo have long since passed the period of youth. Never sparing himself, working night and day, fasting, existing so parsimoniously that he at times well nigh offended that virtue which is next to godliness, he lived to the age of eighty-nine years, retaining his powers but little impaired unto the last. During his residence in Bologna, according to his own statement, he lived in one wretched room with three laborers who were assisting him with his work, the four occupying one bed. For some undiscoverable reason none of them died with the plague which was prevalent that summer. Michael considerately suggested to his brother, who spoke of paying him a visit, that he was a trifle short on space, and accom-

modations for five in one small room with one bed were none
of the best, the sequel being that his brother nobly resisted
the temptation to visit him. The great painter was in some
respects not a brave man. There were times in his life that
he lived in mortal terror of assassination, and even con-
templated fleeing to Constantinople because of his imaginary
fear of the Pope, the last person who thought of doing him
harm.

We have anticipated a little in recording some things
at the beginning of our study relating to Angelo's life, but
we have done so that a better understanding may be had of
the singular character of the creative genius who stands to
the Latin race, as Shakspere does to the Anglo-Saxon, a
giant in power and magnitude. Angelo had a quick and
violent temper and was easily provoked to quarrel. He
worked always with feverish energy. We have the testimony
of an eye-witness that even after he was past sixty he could
knock off more chips from extremely hard marble in fifteen
minutes than three young and muscular stone cutters could
in three or four hours. "He put such impetuosity and fury
into his work," the same witness continues, "that I thought
the whole must fly to pieces! hurling to the ground at one
blow great fragments three or four inches thick, shaving the
line so closely that if he had overpassed it by a hair's breadth
he ran the risk of losing all." He was absolutely insensible
to everything which is usually regarded as luxurious in life,
such things, for example, as jewels, dress, flowers, beauty of
scenery and landscapes. He ate only because it was necessary and not because he enjoyed the taste of food. When
he was at work upon any of his great creations he ate only a
piece of bread and that while he was working. He slept but
little, reclining often without removing his clothes or boots;
sleep, according to his own statement, especially an excessive
amount, nearly always deranged his stomach. When he slept

at all he went immediately from his work to rest. He was
the genius of labor incarnate and could not be idle for a
moment. For many years he was the mainstay of his family,
supporting his father and brothers with whom he frequently
quarreled, at the same time sacrificing his comforts for theirs.
His outlook on life was always serious, never frivolous, his
temperament in this respect belonging to the northern races
rather than to the southern. He outlived eleven popes, and
during his lifetime more important events happened than
in any other hundred years of the world's history.

This man, so peculiar in his habits of life, so sombre and
melancholy in his disposition, was the most universal genius
that ever lived. He was the greatest sculptor and, in his own
line, the greatest painter of modern times. He was also a
very great architect and a poet of high order. No other
genius of the first rank can lay claim to so many excellencies.
Leonardo, who in sheer intellectual daring surpassed him, as
he did all of mankind, lacked the close application of Angelo
and consequently has left no adequate monuments to his
name. Raphael's genius was saner, if less sublime, but he
was a painter only. Michael Angelo's work was so varied
and so enormous that to get even the most inadequate idea of
it in a short study, it must be approached in some sort of
systematic way. As he was preeminently a sculptor, his
painting even being sculpturesque in style, it is perhaps better to consider first his work in that field.

There are twenty-three or twenty-four extant productions of his in sculpture, the greatest being the *Pieta* in St.
Peters at Rome, the *David* in the Academy at Florence, the
Tomb of Pope Julius II., including the *Moses* in St. Pietro
in Vincola in Rome, the *Medici chapel sculptures* in the
church of San Lorenzo, Florence, and the two slaves designed
originally for the tomb of Pope Julius. There are several
other exceedingly valuable pieces, particularly the *Bacchus*

in the National Museum at Florence, the *Cupid* in the South Kensington Museum at London and the *Madonna* in the church of Notre Dame at Bruges, but none of these is so preeminently great as are the others mentioned.

When we first enter St. Peters we experience an uncanny feeling of awe, something, I doubt not, like we should feel if suddenly transported by some miraculous power to a Brobdignagian world where the dimensions of everything appeared to be tenfold greater than that of the world with which we were familiar. This is a totally inadequate description of the feeling one has when he confronts the *Pieta* in St. Peters, Angelo's first great work in marble. Seated on a stone at the foot of the Cross, gazing intently and sadly upon his wounds, the Virgin Mother, the youngest of all Angelo's women, is represented as holding the dead Christ in her arms. Angelo was severely criticised by some for not making her older; whereupon he declared that the Mother of God was no ordinary woman and might well appear younger than she really was. The dead Christ is inexpressibly beautiful, the hands and feet are perfectly modeled and with the utmost delicacy, and the religious spirit of the statue is superb. Shortly after it was put in its place it was witness to one of the most shocking scenes recorded in the bloody annals of the times. Alexander VI., the most infamous pope who ever filled the papal chair, had paid the penalty of his crimes, and his dead body, the most repulsive, monstrous and deformed corpse, according to Villari, which had ever been seen, was carried by six porters and two carpenters to the chapel, where, at the foot of Angelo's *Pieta,* it was packed into a rudely constructed coffin. This grewsome work was done at night with the aid only of two torches which cast two weird and ghostly beams into the otherwise total darkness. The coffin had been made too narrow and too short for the body, a defect not regarded by the brutal workmen, who, with ghastly jeers and still more ghastly jests, denuded the dead pope of his tiara and robes of office, wrapped the body in an old carpet and then, as Villari relates, "with force of fists and feet rammed it down into the box. There was not a ministering priest, not a single attendant, not a consecrated candle." Thus, all night long the dead Christ and his sorrowing mother kept solitary vigil beside the blackened corpse of their degenerate vicar upon earth.

The *Statue of David,* now in the Academy of the Fine Arts at Florence, is a young colossus, in which Angelo first exhibited that mastery of the sublime which he never after surrendered. This statue was cut out of a huge block of marble which another sculptor had abandoned because he found it too hard to work. The statue, though enormous and powerful, lacks grace, and is, as Wolfbin with German frankness puts it, "positively ugly." The hands are large and awkward and the feet ample enough to support a cathedral. Its strength, as a work of art, consists in the majestic poise of the head and the tense dramatic attitude of the body. One imagines that in another moment this tremendous athlete will send the stone he holds in his left hand crashing through the brain of the Philistine giant. The people of Florence originally set this statue up in the largest square of the city immediately in front of the Palazzo Vecchio where it stood for over three hundred years, until, in 1873, it was moved to its present position in the Academy of the Fine Arts. Vasari relates that after it had been finished Piero Soderini, the gonfalonier, told Angelo that the statue was perfect except the nose which was too large; whereupon Michael, not wishing to offend the city dignitary, who, of course, knew nothing about such things, managed to let some marble dust fall on Soderini; the latter, thinking it came from chiseling on the nose, told the artist that he had now "given it life."

The *Tomb of Pope Julius* was the nightmare of the artist, and has since become the nightmare of his biographers and critics. This tragedy, as it has well been called, began in 1505 and ended in 1545 in a state of titanic incompleteness. As originally planned the work was to be set up in the Tribune of St. Peters, and had it been carried out, as it could have been had not the inexcusable pigheadedness of certain succeeding pontiffs interfered, it would have been the greatest wonder of the modern world. More than forty statues were required for the original plan, only a few of which were ever completed, these few being Angelo's greatest contribution to sculpture. The most prominent among these statues is his *Moses* which now stands in the church of San Pietro in Vincola. Next to the *Moses* are the two slaves now in the Louvre at Paris. The *Moses* is one of those works of art which impresses the beholder powerfully at first sight, then somewhat unfavorably, and it is only after all of the conflicting emotions subside that the heart awards to this tremendous creation the full measure of homage. One of the oldest of Angelo's biographers has written thus about it:

"Worthy of all admiration is the *Statue of Moses,* duke and captain of the Hebrews. He sits posed in the attitude of a thinker and a sage, holding beneath his left arm the tables of the law, and with the left hand giving support to his chin, like one who is tired and full of anxious cares. From the fingers of this hand escape long flowing lines of beard, which are very beautiful in their effect upon the eye. The face is full of vivid life and spiritual force, fit to inspire both love and terror as perhaps the man in truth did. It is a marvellous work and full of art."

In the presence of this sublime masterpiece we experience a feeling like that expressed by a countryman of Angelo's a hundred years after his death:

" 'Tis Moses when he left the Mount with part
Of God's eternal glory round him thrown."

Nowhere else can we find such majesty of soul in marble as we discover here.

The two slaves in the Louvre, originally intended for the *Tomb of Julius,* are among the most notable productions of Michael Angelo. The one with his hand thrown back over his head is the most fascinatingly beautiful of all his creations. He is a youth of exquisite shape, a Renaissance Mercury or Apollo with a new and triumphant spirit infused into his body. Symonds said that "It is impossible while gazing on this statue not to hear a strain of intellectual music. Indeed, like melody it tells no story, awakes no desire, but fills the soul with something beyond thought or passion, subtler and more penetrating than words."

In 1524, while the tragedy of Julius was still being enacted, Michael Angelo received an order for a statue of Christ triumphant, an order which he did not fill until seven years later. This work does not seem to have interested him and he committed it to an assistant, Pietro Vibano, to finish. His friend, the Venetian painter, Sebastian del Piombo, wrote to him that the work was not getting on well. "He," speaking of Vibano, "has spoiled the marble wherever he has touched it. In particular he has shortened the right foot and cut the toes off. It is clear also that he has been peddling at the beard, and I believe my little boy would have done it with more sense, for it looks as though he used a knife without a point to chisel the hair. This can easily be remedied, however. He has also spoiled one of the nostrils. A little more and the whole nose would have been ruined and only God could have restored it." The statue is the object of very exaggerated religious devotion. A brass shoe has been put on the right foot to keep it from being entirely kissed away by its devout worshippers. Critics differ as to its artistic

value, some ranking it with *Moses,* others regarding it as an
inferior piece of work. It is certainly, however, a most singular conception of the Christ. He stands erect holding the
cross which is planted by his side, and the curling locks and
warrior-like expression are anything but divine. What a
travesty it seems compared with Leonardo's Christ in the
Last Supper! Neither Michael Angelo nor Raphael ever
caught a vision of the Son of God such as da Vinci's. Not
that they were not religious but their religion possessed elements which somehow obscured their view of what was most
divine in the Christ face. Fundamentally, Angelo was more
a Hebrew and Raphael more a Greek than they were Chris-
tians.

Next to the tragedy of the *Tomb of Julius* in the life
of Michael Angelo we place the tragedy of the Medici Chapel
in Florence. In this prolonged but incomparably majestic
creation we see the culmination of the sculptor's genius. The
tombs of two of the house of the Medici, Giuliano, the
brother, and Lorenzo, the grandson, of Lorenzo the Magnificent, are made immortal in marble. Beneath each of the
two statues of the princes are the recumbent figures of a
man and woman called Twilight and Dawn, and Night and
Day. Looking upon these voiceless creations one feels
hushed and awed as in the presence of some sublime revelation given through means hitherto unknown to man. Lorenzo in his place above the prostrate figures of Twilight and
Dawn sits with his hand beneath his chin in perpetual meditation, some have thought, over the ruin of his house, some
of the coming desolation of Italy and some over the uncer-
tainties of life in general. Opposite him, on the other side
of the chapel, sits Giuliano with face less solemn and melancholy, though no less majestic, and with arm ready for action,
while at his feet recline the figures of Night and Day, the
latter partly unchiseled.

What does all this mean? has been the question asked and answered by every student of Michael Angelo during the last four centuries. The answers have been almost without number, most of them refering to some criticism of the house of the Medici or to some contemporary event. Unless one has a distinctly historical bias I do not believe that these solutions will satisfy. Michael Angelo was preeminently a thinker and an artist and concerned himself little with political questions or problems. He was tremendously interested in life in general and very little concerned in things distinctly patriotic or purely national. His mind was too great for one nation or country. That these creations, in a certain sense the culminating work of his life, allude to the fortunes of any one house or nation, I do not believe; they are rather the contributions he has made in sculpture to the problems of human existence, as the Sistine frescoes are contributions in painting to the same problems. It must be kept constantly in mind that Angelo was above all else an artist, and that the art instinct, no less than the philosophic or prophetic, was always present in his works. The nude human figures, such as we find here, were his means of conveying an impression of the beautiful, which motive alone without anything deeper might account for their creation—it might, but I do not think it does. It seems to me, remembering that Angelo was a thinker as well as an artist, that he has portrayed the two opposite moods, Action and Uncertainty, which are, at one time or another, dominant in every human soul. Lorenzo in meditation watches above the figures of Twilight and Dawn which typify the transition periods from positive night to positive day or from positive day to positive night. On the other side of the chapel and opposite Lorenzo, the one who meditates, sits Giuliano with free hand and expressive eye, no longer meditating but acting, while Night unconsciously sleeps and Day watches with open eyes. Are not these the common moods of humanity, and were these not especially the moods of Michael Angelo? This most arduous and indefatigable worker had his hours and days of gloomy meditation when he pondered almost morbidly over the problems of existence.

The faces of all four figures are serious and solemn, that of the Dawn being the most tragic of the group. Why did Michael Angelo make the transition from night to day, symbolized by the figure of Dawn, more painful than the transition from day to night, symbolized by the figure of Twilight? This question is not difficult to answer by any one who has studied the history of Angelo. Harassed by poverty and ceaseless toil, driven from task to task by Medici princes and Roman popes, weighed down by a constitutional melancholy, with no sweetheart, wife or child to drive it away, constantly seeing his most cherished ambitions blasted by the stupidity of those in authority, was it any wonder that the sublime and lovely face of Dawn should be contorted with agony as she awakens to the torture of life? Michael Angelo, like all genuinely artistic natures, was a bundle of nerves, and as he was cut off by a constitutional peculiarity from most of the joys of life, caring nothing for flowers, ornaments, the pleasures of the table or of any of the senses, his nerves were principally of use to him as a source of suffering.

His Twilight is a figure equally expressive as that of Dawn. He is represented as an old man gazing with downcast eyes, solemn countenance and reflective mien, but with no such expression of torture as is chiseled upon the face of Dawn. The day is almost ended and his task is almost done. He is not quite sure that he has done it as well as it should have been done, but it is a satisfaction to know that it will soon be over. The opposite figure, Night, sleeps in quietude and peace, her hand touching her head and her chin resting upon her breast. Day, like an unfinished Titan, gazes boldly but with no smile of joy upon his face, as he turns it half unwillingly to the sun. The chapel of San Lorenzo is a great study, and no thinking person is ever quite the same after seeing it.

In the Duomo at Florence, behind the high altar, is a group of four persons representing the *Deposition from the Cross,* which is the name of the piece and Angelo's last work in marble. At this time, being over eighty-seven years of age, he suffered from sleeplessness and he was wont frequently to leave his bed at night and work on this statue, wearing a thick paper cap in which he placed a lighted candle made of goat's tallow. One night he hewed so furiously and struck so deeply into the marble that he spoiled the Madonna's elbow. Enraged by his mistake he picked up a hammer and attempted to destroy the whole creation, but fortunately one of his friends begged it of him and having collected the broken pieces it was afterwards restored. It is a sublime creation even yet, and would have made a much more fitting monument (he had planned it for his own sepulchre) than the lifeless one Vasari raised over his tomb in the church of Santa Croce. Between the *Pieta* of St. Peters, the greatest church in Rome, and this broken *Pieta* of the Duomo, the greatest church in Florence, lay sixty years of labor. It was fitting that the life of one so inescapably melancholy should begin and end with the saddest story in the Christian religion.

Great as was Michael Angelo in the realm of sculpture, he is best known and will be remembered longest as a painter. Only one easel picture, the *Holy Family,* now in the Tribuna of the Uffizi, remains from his hand. It is a striking and powerful production but as far from being beautiful as can well be imagined. Joseph and Mary are both rugged peasants, and the Christ child, sturdy and stout, has no touch of the divine about him.   The background, instead of being filled in with trees or houses or woodland scenery of some kind, as Botticelli, Ghirlandajo or Raphael would have prefered, consists of nude youths with no other significance than just to furnish a background.   Besides the *Holy Family* there is one picture in the Pitti Gallery, the design of which was furnished by Angelo, though the picture itself was painted by Rosso Fiorentino.   It is entitled the *Fates,* and is decidedly the most unique work upon that subject in existence.   The three Fates are represented as three old women, Clotho, who holds the distaff, Lachesis, who spins the thread of life, and Atropos, who cuts it with the fatal shears.   The little poem called *Villa Franca,* by James Russell Lowell, contains the following refrain:

> "Spin, spin, Clotho, spin!
> Lachesis, twist! and Atropos sever!
> In the shadow, year out, year in,
> The silent headsman waits forever."

The most noticeable thing about the picture is that while the attitudes and, in a sense, the faces differ, yet the features are in reality the same.   The immortal artist and thinker discerns beneath all semblances that however different life and its destiny may appear to be they are in truth the same.   The happiest hour and the saddest hour of our careers are linked together and however diverse the threads of our existence may seem to be, it is the same fate which spins and cuts the thread of life.

Before we come to what is far and away the greatest work of Michael Angelo in painting, the all but indescribable frescoes of the Sistine Chapel, we should speak briefly of his cartoon of the *Soldiers Bathing,* his first picture, and painted, in competition with Leonardo's *Battle of the Standard,* for the side walls of the council chamber of the Palazzo

The Three Fates   *Florence*

By Michael Angelo

Vecchio at Florence. Cellini, a good judge, says of this picture:

"Nothing survives of ancient or modern times which touches the same lofty point of excellence, and, as I have already said, the design of the great Leonardo was itself most admirably beautiful. These two cartoons stood, the one in the palace of the Medici, the other in the hall of the Pope. So long as they remained intact they were the school of the world."

Cellini even goes so far as to say that they were superior to the Sistine frescoes, to quote his own words, "the latter did not rise half way to the same pitch of power." This picture represented a number of foot soldiers bathing in the Arno when the alarm for battle was sounded. The hasty scramble of the soldiers for arms and clothing furnished Angelo with a rare opportunity for that display of muscle and sinew in which he so much delighted. Both of these pictures, Leonardo's and Angelo's, have long since been destroyed, their power being judged only by scattered fragments of engravings. Though all else should perish, the Sistine Chapel remains a monument to the Titan of Florence.

It is with a feeling of the utter inadequacy of the power of language to describe the Sistine frescoes that I undertake the task, in which attempt I ask for the utmost assistance that the reader's imagination can give, particularly those readers who have not seen the Sistine Chapel. Imagine a large rectangular room approximately forty-five yards in length, fifteen in breadth and twenty-three in height, the two ends of which are flat surfaces, the western end being covered with Angelo's tremendous fresco of the *Last Judgment* and the eastern end with ten paintings by an artist of less power. The room is lighted by twelve windows, six on each side, high up toward the ceiling. Beneath these windows are twelve frescoes, mostly episodes in the life of Moses painted by

Botticelli, Ghirlandajo, Roselli, Perugino and one or two others of lesser note. The high altar is at the western end, to the left of which, facing Botticelli's fresco of the *Temptation,* is the papal throne and opposite the tribune for the choir used during Holy Week. This is the Sistine Chapel, used for the conclave of cardinals in the election of a pope, and is by long odds the most famous chapel in Christendom.

What concerns us particularly is the ceiling of this famous shrine which contains the frescoes of Michael Angelo. It took him about four and one half years to complete these frescoes, covering, as they do, over ten thousand square feet of surface. In the middle of the ceiling are nine large pictures in splendidly subdued coloring, on either side of which are five much larger ones, on the one side three men and two women and on the other three women and two men. There is also, at either end, a large picture of a man, which, combined with the five on either side, make, as it were, an ocean of line and color surrounding a continent comprised of nine of the most tremendous paintings of their kind ever conceived in the brain and fashioned by the hand of man. These twelve pictures which surround the nine are pictures of seven prophets and five sibyls.

The Sistine ceiling should be studied from the western end of the room just behind the high altar. Observed from this station, the first of the nine pictures in the middle represents a gigantic figure in a sort of elemental chaos, called the *Separation of Light from Darkness,* and the most extraordinary representation of that tremendous fiat "Let there be light" which has ever been conceived by the imagination of genius. The second picture, immediately following, called the *Creation of the Sun and Moon,* is double the length of the first, and this alternation, which continues across the ceiling, results in five short and four long pictures. The picture of the *Creation of the Sun and Moon* represents two figures

Creation of the Sun and Moon, Sistine Ceiling
By Michael Angelo

whirling through space, conveying such a vivid sense of power and motion combined as, I believe, no other picture in the world can rival. The third picture, another short one, is a representation of the Spirit of the Lord brooding over the water. The fourth, which is a long one, is the *Creation of Adam,* a picture of an old man touching with his finger the outstretched hand of the first man, awaking from the elemental clay. This figure of Adam is justly regarded as Michael Angelo's embodiment in painting of his ideal of physical manhood. The fifth, a shorter one, is the *Creation of Eve* from the side of Adam, one of the most beautiful pictures of the nine. As Adam is Angelo's ideal man so Eve is incomparably his ideal woman. He seems for the time to have forgotten his dislike for women in painting the Mother of the race, though even here Angelo is infinitely below Titian's perfection of feminine form. Following the *Creation of Woman,* is the sixth picture, which represents the *Fall of Man.* The face of Satan is marvelously fair to look upon as he offers Eve "the fruit of the Tree," though his body ends in the foul coils of the serpent. The seventh, another short picture, shows Noah at sacrifice, and the eighth, the last long one, is a picture of the *Universal Deluge.* This one is crowded with figures and does not seem to harmonize perfectly with the scale of the others. The ninth and last represents the *Sin of Ham and the Drunkenness of Noah.* This series of pictures from the *Fall of Man* is a sort of anti-climax, if I may use the term, not in execution but in subject, and this is in harmony with the Bible account of the decadence of man from his original glory. Even so, the sublimity and majesty in these four frescoes are unequalled, the entire series, representing, as it does, the creation of the world and of man, the entrance of sin into this newly created world and its first great catastrophe in the universal deluge, is the most tremendous conception in all the history of genius.

Having briefly described this continent of frescoes, we will now with corresponding brevity, refer to the ocean of line and color which surrounds it. At the western end of the Sistine ceiling, over the high altar and extending back of it to the point where the observer is standing, is a large picture of Jonah. Beginning now with this fresco, the first picture on the left (remember the observer is facing the eastern end of the chapel) is that of the prophet Jeremiah, the next that of the Persian sibyl, said to have been the first to prophesy the coming of Christ; this is followed by the prophet Ezekiel, succeeded immediately by the Erythraean sibyl, living, according to Pausanias, anterior to the Trojan War, which she predicted. The picture following this one is that of the prophet Joel, which completes the left side of the ceiling, all of which taken together make five portraits, three of men and two of women.

At the eastern end of the ceiling is the picture of the prophet Zechariah, the fifth of the seven prophets represented. Beginning now with this fresco of Zechariah, the first picture on the right is that of the Delphian sibyl, the most beautiful and, according to Plutarch, the first of all. With the possible exception of the sibyl of Cumae, she is perhaps more widely known than any others of the ten enumerated by Varro. After her succeeds the perfect picture of the prophet Isaiah, followed by the famous Cumaean sibyl, the prophetess it will be remembered, of whom Aeneas inquired the way to Hades. She is also the one who offered to sell the nine sibylline Books to Tarquin the Proud, the seventh and last King of Rome, who, though refusing to buy the nine and later the six, afterwards bought the remaining three for the same price she had asked for the nine. The picture of the Cumaean sibyl is succeeded by Daniel, the last of the prophets, which is followed by that of the Libyan sibyl, the oldest of all the sibyls, as related in Pausanias. This

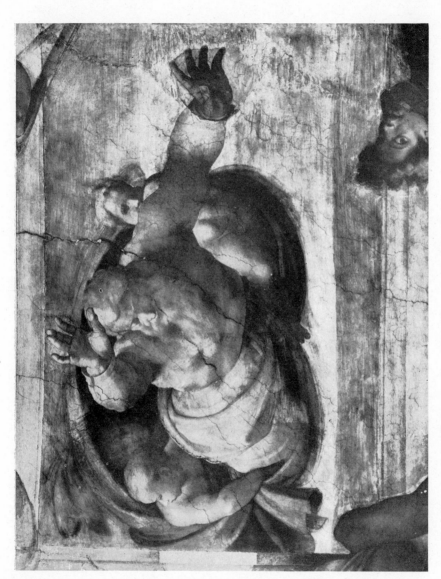

The Spirit of the Lord Brooding Over the Waters, Sistine Ceiling
By Michael Angelo

is the last painting on the right next to that of Jonah at
the western end, making the five pictures, three of women
and two of men, and completing the ocean of color that surrounds the continent of the nine central pictures.

What we have so inadequately told is but half of what
Michael Angelo has accomplished in the vault of the Sistine.
The portraits mentioned are not isolated, but are fitted into
spaces made for them in a vast architectural frame work
which is painted on the ceiling. On the edges and corners of
this frame work, in short, everywhere that he was given
the slightest chance, Michael Angelo painted gigantic
nude slaves or genii, as they have been called, tremendous
beings, with large muscular limbs, small heads and, for the
most part, expressionless faces. Just what he meant by
these figures it would be hard to say, but they seem to have
been the object of his especial delight and care.

We have referred to Angelo's preference for masculine
beauty and his aversion to feminine. Here in the vault of
the Sistine he has given the most positive expression to this
feeling, going as far as he could go in painting. Strangely
enough, Angelo never even mentions his mother, though
refering so frequently to his father. This almost total lack
of appreciation of woman has been one reason that modern
scientific experts have offered in support of their contention
that Michael Angelo was not sane. The truth is that the
genius of this mighty sculptor was essentially of the masculine, the stern, powerful and sublime type, to which he
devoted his entire thought and energy, finding no time for
the gentler virtues or pleasures, even had he been so inclined.
He had not the courtly grace of Leonardo, the delicate,
refined and ideal fancies of Botticelli, nor the kindly gentle
ways of Raphael which drew all hearts to him. Rather did
the stern Titan prefer to live alone in the solitary grandeur
of the clouds, surrounded by the lightnings and thunders of

the elemental chaos and admitting none of earth's denizens to his abode. To the heights where avalanches crash, to whose tempestuous glories lesser souls could not aspire; these thunder-riven peaks seemed to be the home of Angelo's soul. How could such a man either understand or love woman or be loved by her?

Michael Angelo's *Last Judgment,* covering the western end of the Sistine Chapel, is the largest fresco in the world. He was between sixty and sixty-five years old when he painted this picture, or more than twenty years after he had finished the ceiling. The first impression of this fresco, when seen from the east end or centre of the room, is that of a confused mass of figures, which gradually assume definite form and place, and out of the chaos one tremendous form seems to rise in the centre, which, with outstretched arms and threatening gesture, hurls vengeance upon the unhappy wretches sinking down into Tartarus. Terrible looking creatures, one pierced with arrows, one flayed alive, another with a wheel of torture and others with harrows, racks and other hellish devices, flourish these various symbols of torment, all seeming to implore the Judge to avenge them upon their enemies. There is not a note of consolation or joy in the real sense anywhere, not even in the comparatively small part of the picture devoted to the blest. The Judge does not seem at all like the Christ of Leonardo. Vengeance, not mercy, is Angelo's conception of the Judgment—the kind in which every orthodox Christian of those times believed. The *Last Judgment* was severely criticised when first painted because of its supra-offensive realism, a fault which has been rectified ethically though hardly esthetically, for the painters employed to do the work were bad colorists. Biagio, Master of Ceremonies in the Vatican, complained to Pope Paul of this too realistic picture of the medieval conception of the Judgment, a criticism which so enraged Angelo that the

Detail of the Creation of Man   By Michael Angelo   *Rome*

next day he painted the carping Biagio in the lowest circle of hell with horns on his head and a snake wrapped around his loins. When Biagio again complained to Paul the latter told him that if Michael had put him in purgatory he might have procured his release, but having put him in hell there was no hope of getting him out.

There is a point to this criticism of Biagio. Michael Angelo was not immoral, he was non-moral, his whole soul being so filled with the esthetic ideal that he did not think of the ethical one way or the other. For this reason some of his work, from an ethical standpoint, must be condemned. This is particularly true of one of his statues in the Bargillo in Florence and of a painting on the same subject which, we are told, nauseated even a French inspector and was on that account destroyed.

As an architect, Michael is best known by the superb dome of St. Peters, the greatest thing of its kind in the world. Strictly speaking, he was not a builder and his work elsewhere in architecture, as, for example, the Laurentian Library in Florence, is not exceptionally creditable. But the cupola of St. Peters is as great a creation, in its own way, as the Medici tombs or the Sistine Chapel. One of his critics has said of this work:

"The circle which it describes finds no phrase of language to express its grace. It is neither ellipse nor parabola nor a section of the circle, but an inspiration of creative fancy."

He was eighty-two years old when he made the model, and it was his last great work. During all the time he was engaged in this task he refused to accept pecuniary compensation of any kind for his services, in striking contrast with the corrupt covetousness so prevalent at the time.

Not only was Michael Angelo a supremely great sculptor and painter and the author of at least one incomparably

sublime achievement in architecture, but he was also a poet
of no little distinction, much of his writing being very highly
esteemed by his people.   His verse is mostly confined to the
sonnet, very popular in his time.   A large number of his
sonnets are addressed to two people, Vittoria Colonna and
Tommaso Cavalieri, whose names his biographers have frequently associated with his own.   There has been a great deal
of nonsense written about his relations with Vittoria Colonna, in spite of all that has been said about his sonnets
furnishing evidence for such a romance.   Vittoria Colonna
was undoubtedly a friend of the painter—perhaps the only
woman who ever was his friend, but the gossip which some
assiduous biographers, intent upon finding a romance in
Michael Angelo's life, have thrown around the famous
painter and Vittoria is of thin air, vanishing at the touch of
criticism.   His expressions, poetical or otherwise, are not so
violent or so evidently sincere as those written about the loss
of his old servant Vibino.   There is nothing indicating excessive grief in these simple words written after her death:

> "She felt the warmest affection for me, and I
> no less for her.   Death has robbed us of a great
> friend."

He even uses the masculine gender in the word "friend"—
un grande amico.   Imagine Romeo speaking of Juliet as
un grande amico.   In the case of Michael Angelo, however,
it is only just to say that the use of the masculine gender
was an evidence of his superior regard.   One of his sonnets
to her, I think the most lovely of all of them, has this
thought:

> "A man within a woman, nay, a god,
>   Speaks through her spoken word;
>   I, therefore, who have heard,
>   Must suffer change, and shall be mine no more.
>   She lured me from the paths I whilom trod,
>   Borne from my former state by her away,

> I stand aloof and mine own self deplore.
> Above all vain desire
> The beauty of her face doth lift my clay;
> All lesser loveliness seems charnel mire.
> O lady, who through fire
> And water leadest souls to joy eterne,
> Let me no more unto myself return."

There is a touch of Romeo's ardor in her leading him "through fire and water," but the words "a man within a woman" and "above all vain desire" neutralize, if they do not wholly dissipate, the passion. In connection with the alleged Vittoria Colonna romance, it may be worth while to note that Michael Angelo was sixty-three and Vittoria approximately fifty when they first met.

Whatever his devotion to Vittoria Colonna may have been, his affection for Tommaso Cavalieri, a young Italian, was equally pronounced, and the sonnets addressed to him equally ardent, as ardent, indeed, as those which Shakspere addressed to Mr. W. H. This was a prevailing fashion of the time, quite independent of any peculiar individual constitution, such as Angelo's.

Speaking of his poetry, one of his finest sonnets is a lament for his youth, gone beyond recall:

> "Ah me! ah me! how have I been betrayed
> By my swift flitting years, and by the glass
> Which yet tells truth to those who firmly gaze!
> Thus happens it when one too long delays,
> As I have done, nor feels time fleet and fade.
> One morn he finds himself grown old, alas!
> To gird my loins, repent, my path repass,
> Sound counsel take, I cannot, now death's near,
> Life to myself, each tear,
> Each sigh is idly to the light wind sent,
> For there's no loss to equal time ill spent."

Surely the man "who rounded Peter's dome," who chiseled the *Moses* and the *David,* who spent at intervals forty years in carving the colossal tragedies represented in the *Tombs of Pope Julius* and the *Medici,* to say nothing of the sublimities of the Sistine Chapel, seems to have little cause to speak of "time ill spent." Perhaps what he means is expressed in the concluding lines of the second stanza:

> "Far from the truth my steps have gone astray;
>   On peril now I stay,
>   For lo! the brief span of my life is o'er,
>   Yet, were it lengthened, I should love once more."

Only a brief summing up of Michael Angelo's work is all that remains to be done in concluding this study. The final expression of Leonardo was the woman of mystery, not the earthly virgin or mother but womanhood in the abstract —the face of Mona Lisa. To a genius so delicate and yet withal so penetrating as his, this was the ultimate problem. Botticelli, the victim of peculiar circumstances, saw his ultimate problem likewise in the face of a woman—not the woman of Leonardo with her clear, calm, unfathomable serenity, but rather the wan, pale Madonna of the *Magnificat,* typifying that longing for the ideal and dissatisfaction with the actual which it was his lot to experience so bitterly. But Michael Angelo struck out along totally different lines, not only from these but from all subsequent painters. The ultimate problem with him was masculine rather than feminine. His ideals were all masculine, his style and manner sublime, terrible, awe-inspiring, never possessing supreme delicacy or grace. He was impatient with landscape decoration or any other artistic device or material, where they could be used at all, aside from the bodies of men. In almost every case, too, he reversed the modern conception that the face is the all essential thing in the artistic personality. The body appeals more strongly to him than the features. As an instance of this, observe those genii in the vault of the Sistine Chapel. Their expressions are singularly blank and abstract, but what care has been taken with the poise of limb and body, what extreme effort to make the physical bulk appeal to us on that account alone with the result that it does so appeal. He was distinctively the prophet of the sublime, and his works have all the awe-inspiring power of a message from the lightnings and thunders of some new Sinai over which he broods supreme. He was a disciple of the gospel of toil, and few human beings have labored so terribly as he. In many ways he resembles the greatest of England's epic poets—Milton. To him, as well as to Milton, Wordsworth's superb lines apply:

> "Thy soul was as a star and dwelt apart,
> Thou hadst a voice whose sound was like the sea."

The sublime epic of *Paradise Lost* is truly as the sound of the sea, but not more so than those tremendous epics in the Sistine Chapel. Leonardo was a dramatic, Angelo an epical, painter. He lives and moves and has his being in the old days of myths and demigods, and is not at home in even medieval Italy. As *Paradise Lost* may be likened to the Sistine frescoes, so the *Last Judgment* may be likened to *Samson Agonistes*. Both are terribly dramatic epics, both terribly sublime, but both have the seal of decay upon them. We will carry the parallel no farther. Michael Angelo was more than Milton because he was so many-sided, but whether he, or any other, was greater so far as he went, admits of question.

Michael Angelo was constitutionally gloomy and depressed. He continually deplored the paucity of his achievements and what he regarded as his failure to make the best of his opportunities. It is true, though through no fault of his, that much of his time was wasted as a result of the stupidity of the popes and others for whom he worked. Really to understand the meaning of the quiet repose of

Night and the agonized waking of Dawn in the chapel of San Lorenzo, is to understand Michael Angelo, or, conversely, to understand him is to understand what they mean. Tired of the futile, restless, feverish struggle of life, he fell into the dreamless sleep at 5 o'clock of the evening of the 18th of February, 1564, having made his will in three sentences, in which he committed his soul to God, his body to the earth and his substance to his nearest relatives. Does not the following sonnet of his, so beautifully translated by Wordsworth, help us to interpret the great figure of Night in San Lorenzo and tell us of his own longing for her peace?

"Grateful is Sleep, my life in stone bound fast;
More grateful still; while wrong and shame shall last,
On me can Time no happier state bestow
Than to be left unconscious of the woe.
Ah then, lest you awaken me, speak low.

"Grateful is Sleep, more grateful still to be
Of marble; for while shameless wrong and woe
Prevail, 'tis best to neither hear nor see.
Then wake me not, I pray you. Hush, speak low.

"Come, gentle Sleep, Death's image tho' thou art,
Come share my couch, nor speedily depart;
How sweet thus living without life to lie,
Thus without death how sweet it is to die."

RAPHAEL

. . .

The Shakspere of Art

RAPHAEL

No greater contrast can be imagined than that between Raphael and Michael Angelo. Refined and delicate in his habits, kind and gentle to all, disarming even his rivals with praise for their work and self-depreciation of his own, Raphael had the most successful career in the history of art, and more tears of sincere sorrow were shed over his grave than over those of all his contemporaries put together. He was handsome in appearance, not with the god-like features of Goethe or the classic head of Byron, but with such refinement of expression and sweetness of manner that he unconsciously drew all hearts to his own. He loved beautiful things and, unlike Michael Angelo, he delighted in fine and handsome clothes, in ornaments and jewels. While the immortal Angelo lived on bread and water and occupied the same room with his workmen, Raphael, though by no means wealthy, for he was an orphan child, dressed as costly as he could, ate meat and seasoned his water with wine. He worshiped his mother Magia Santi, though she died when he was but a small boy, and his sublimest and sweetest creations are idealizations of motherhood; Michael Angelo, on the contrary, as we have indicated, never mentions his mother. Angelo was quarrelsome and high-tempered, never able to get along with his workmen, his family or his friends, while Raphael attached every one to him and never had an enemy except those who envied him his genius and success. He died at the age of thirty-seven leaving behind him much material for romantic stories. Chivalry was inborn in Raphael and the spirit of knighthood was in his blood. At the age of twenty he painted his celebrated *Spousal of the Virgin,* in which he departed from the practice of his master Perugino by giving the place of honor to the bridesmaids of Mary, a place hitherto always given to men in paintings. To do this was in defiance of one of the time-honored canons of art, but so thoroughgoing was his chivalric nature that he did not hesitate.

Perhaps we of a later day are prone to love the handsome, knightly Umbrian more than we do the solitary Titan of Florence, and our justification for this preference is obvious. It should nevertheless be kept in mind that Michael reached heights of which Raphael perhaps never dreamed, and, though far less objective in his genius, remains, in other respects, the one gigantic, unapproachable figure of his time. Leonardo's genius is like the lightning that flashes in glory across the heavens, Michael Angelo's like the storm clouds which gather around some lofty and inaccessible mountain, far, terrible, sublime, Raphael's like the sunlight or some bright exhalation of the dawn which falls everywhere, illuminating hovel and palace alike, the works of his genius being loved while the works of the others are revered. *Faust, Paradise Lost, Hamlet,* which do we prefer? Our choice, or the choice of most of us, has been the world's. And so will the preference be given in the field of Italian painting. There is something about the names suggestive of the three artists who bore them—Leonardo, the unconquered lion, Michael, the archangel, commander of the angelic hosts in the Almighty's terrific battles with Satan and the apostate angels, Raphael, the kindly courteous messenger of God to man, who talks and eats with Adam in the Garden.

Raphael Sanzio was born in Urbino in central Italy on the evening of April 6, 1483. His father, Giovanni Santi, was a painter of little eminence, who probably taught his son the rudiments of art. Unlike Michael Angelo his mother nursed and personally cared for him. He played, like all the other Italian children of his time and since, in the market place, and perhaps before his father's door watching with delighted childish eyes the figures as they took shape upon the canvas at the touch of the parental brush. Then one October day, in 1491, a little over a year before his great countryman, Columbus, discovered the New World, his mother, Magia Santi, died. He was only a little over eight years old, but he must have remembered her well, for in all that marvelous galaxy of Madonnas which fill the world with his name and fame is there one he painted without some thought or memory of his mother? However this may be, her place in the home was soon to be filled by another, a goldsmith's daughter and little more than a girl. The child and his new mother did not get on well together, and the breach widening more rapidly after his father's death, which occurred three years later, his maternal uncle, observing the young man's remarkable aptitude for painting, sent him to Pietro Perugino, so called because he lived in Perugia. Perugino, whose works are chiefly remembered to-day because of Raphael's fame, was at that time the best teacher in central Italy. He was very avaricious, according to Giorgio Vasari's *Lives of Italian Painters,* an exceedingly quaint and interesting but equally unreliable work. This unreliability of Vasari's biographies is to be deplored, as they are the only contemporary narratives of the life-stories of the Italian painters. At any rate, Vasari records that Perugino was avaricious, an atheist and an unbeliever in the immortality of the soul. He accounts for Perugino's avarice by the hard circumstances of his early life. The painter, he says, was so poor that he was not able to have a bed when he went to Florence to study art but slept on a chest.

Regardless of Perugino's religious beliefs, he had a most decided aptitude and bent for painting religious pic-

tures, especially crucifixions, the best one of all that I know
having been painted by him in the church of Santa Madda-
lena del Pazzi in Florence, and a very powerful picture it is.
Raphael studied under Perugino eight or ten years and the
early works attributed to him all show the influence of the
master. There is the same love of landscape, the same serious
expression, the same peculiar mannerisms. His earliest picture, painted about the age of eighteen, was probably a
crucifixion now in the possession of Lord Dudley, in London. It has the characteristics of Pinturicchio, Signorelli
and Perugino, those of the last named predominating. His
drawing in this picture is not of the best but the genuine
Raphael touch is there in the faces of the Magdalen and
St. Jerome, who look longingly up into the eyes of the
Christ. Raphael's best known picture of this early period
of his life is the *Spousal of the Virgin,* now at Milan. The
idea is, for the most part, borrowed from a similar picture
painted by Perugino for an altarpiece in Caen. The high-
priest stands in the centre and joins the hands of Joseph and
Mary. It has been remarked that Raphael did violence to
antiquity and tradition by giving the place of honor to the
women, a touch of chivalry that he did not learn from
Perugino. One of the bridesmaids is very beautiful and it
is thought that Raphael drew her from life, as there is a
sketch of the same face in Venice. There is another interesting character who is breaking a wand across his knee, apparently a jealous lover of Mary, for he has a decidedly painful
expression on his face, which is accentuated because he is
trying to smile.

Between the close of Raphael's Perugian career and
the beginning of his Florentine there is a picture, now in
the National Gallery, London, which represents a knight
clad in full armor lying asleep at the foot of a tree with
his shield beneath his head. A beautiful woman with a sword

Betrothal of the Virgin   By Raphael   Milan

in one hand and a book in the other stands at his head while another woman, equally beautiful, with a myrtle wreath in her hands stands at his feet. Authorities on art have called this picture the *Dream of a Knight,* the meaning of which they interpret to be the conflict in the mind of a young man between the myrtle wreath of pleasure and the sword of duty. Some have asserted that because the woman, holding the myrtle, is sketched in his Venetian note-book she is not wholly a creature of Raphael's imagination. It is to be doubted, however, whether he would have painted a woman, whom he loved, as a siren. I think his record for gallantry is against such a theory.

Raphael was now about twenty-one years of age and hearing of the great contest going on in Florence between Leonardo da Vinci and Michael Angelo, he decided to move there. This was in 1505. He remained in Florence until 1508 when he was summoned to Rome, these three Florentine years comprising the second period of his career.

When Raphael saw the two great pictures, the *Battle of the Standard* by Leonardo and the *Soldiers Bathing* by Angelo, and came to know the two painters, it did not take him long to choose between them. Anyone who knows anything about Raphael knows also what that choice was. Leonardo's courtly grace, his charming personality, his handsome appearance and kindly courteous manner would attract the gentle, chivalric pupil of Perugino, while the uncouth ways and stern disposition of Michael Angelo would repel him. We can easily imagine the young artist watching with eager interest the completion of these mighty cartoons in the church of Santa Maria Novello. Doubtless he carried away with him impressions and hints which he embodied in his own great battle picture in the Sala di Constantino of the Vatican twelve or fourteen years later. Leonardo's *Battle of the Standard* was the largest picture that had ever been seen in Tuscany, requiring, as it did, over two hundred and eighty-eight square feet of paper and eighty-eight pounds of flour for pasting it. It may be questioned whether any loss in the history of painting can equal the destruction of this cartoon. It was under Leonardo as teacher that Raphael now studied.

Before he left Perugia he had received an order for a Madonna for the nuns of Saint Antonio and had begun painting it. This picture, now in the Metropolitan Museum, New York, was purchased a few years ago by J. Pierpont Morgan for a princely sum, and is remarkable chiefly for revealing, better than any other of Raphael's pictures, the Perugian and Florentine influence. It is very much faded now. Indeed, it was sold by the nuns over two hundred years ago because the surface was flaking off even then. Notwithstanding all this, it is a very interesting Raphael, though not exceptionally beautiful. At the top of the picture the Deity is represented as an aged man with a bald head and a dark forked beard, with a golden globe in his left hand and his right raised in the act of benediction. Underneath, the Virgin sits on an elaborate throne with the infant Saviour on her knee. The child, contrary to custom, is clothed in a white tunic edged with blue and wears a brown belt and blue cloak. He is the most elaborately clad infant in all the round of Italian art. Raphael, as a rule, paints his children nude, but it was one of the requirements in this picture that every figure, including the angels, should be well and completely clad. Even the young John the Baptist, but little over a year old, if that, wears his suit of camel's hair with a robe of purple and gold. The lower part of the picture in its freer expressions illustrates the Florentine manner, while the upper part retains the Umbrian.

From the eight or ten famous Madonnas of Raphael's Florentine period, including among others the *Granduca,*

the *Cardellino,* the *Baldacchino* in Florence, the *Ansidei* in
the National Gallery, the *Madonna in the Garden,* now at
Vienna, the *Casa Tempi* and the *Belle Jardiniere,* I select
four which are really among the most beautiful idealizations
of Christian motherhood in the world. These are the
Granduca, the *Casa Tempi,* the *Belle Jardiniere* and the
Cardellino, the last two being very much alike.

In the *Granduca,* one of the greatest treasures of the
Pitti Gallery in Florence, the expression of divine motherhood has never been surpassed, unless it be in the *Sistine,*
which, I think, only equals it. Though the face is not strikingly beautiful, the hair thin and covered by a veil, the robe
faded and extremely simple, there is perhaps no other picture
ever painted in which the natural love of the mother blends
so perfectly with the feeling of her divine mission or har-
monizes so well with her words in the Magnificat. And the
infant Christ is remarkable, with his wonderful dreamy eyes
looking far away beyond earthly horizons into infinitude.
Before this picture, as before no other, do we feel the full
value and significance of the words: "My soul doth magnify
the Lord." This picture does not impress us immediately;
we may indeed prefer the more attractive, I was about to
say gaudy, *Madonna della Sedia,* which hangs in the same
room, but little by little, like all truly great things, the fascination grows until it becomes almost irresistible. It was the
last picture on which I looked before I left Florence and to
which I said good-by. It is called the *Granduca* because it
once belonged to a Grand Duke Ferdinand of Tuscany
who carried it about with him wherever he went, much as
Alexander the Great did the writings of Homer. The
Granduca is a small picture, two feet three inches and a half
by one foot nine and a half inches, and none in Florence is
worth more in every sense of the term.

The *Madonna di Casa Tempi,* now at Munich, lacks

some of the spiritual depths of the *Granduca,* but no sweeter embodiment of motherly affection was ever imagined. In this picture Raphael is wholly Florentine and in a way that is not seen in the *Granduca.* The Virgin holds her child to her heart and kisses him on the cheek, as he half turns as if to see who is coming. It is likewise a small picture, about two feet four inches high by one foot seven inches wide, and was purchased by King Ludwig of Bavaria in 1829 for 16000 *scudi.*

The *Madonna del Cardellino* and the *Belle Jardiniere,* the one in the Uffizi, the other in the Louvre, differ from the other two mentioned in being larger, in introducing the element of landscape and in adding the figure of St. John as a child. In the *Cardellino,* which was intended for a wedding picture, the Virgin is painted against a background of trees, rural landscape and water with the towers of Florence rising in the distance. At her feet are St. John and the Christ, the former holding a gold-finch, which gives the picture its name, the latter caressing the little captive. St. John with distended cheeks seems out of breath as if he had been running to capture the tiny golden creature, while the Christ calmly and gently caresses it, a touch suggestive of his love and gentleness for all living things. The Madonna is beautiful with that serene and maternal beauty which characterizes nearly all of Raphael's pictures and which fills his dreams with the glory of motherhood. The *Cardellino,* about one and a half times as large as the *Granduca,* was broken into twenty pieces when the Nasi Palace fell in 1547 and was afterwards so skilfully put together that no one but an expert can tell that it was ever injured. The *Belle Jardiniere* is the most important Raphael now in the Louvre. The plan is like that of the *Cardellino* with the same number of figures, the same kind of world-inclusive setting—trees, land, water, the works of man's hands—the same pyramidal

Madonna Della Sedia   *Florence*

By Raphael

arrangement, in short, the same reminiscences of Leonardo.
Added to these things is a greater depth and spirituality of
expression in the face of both Virgin and child which lifts
the later picture above the earlier. The Virgin holds a book
in her hand and St. John carries a lamb in his arms instead
of a gold-finch; aside from this difference in detail the pictures are essentially alike. The *Belle Jardiniere* originally
belonged to the King of Holland, but it afterward came into
the possession of a Frenchman who bequeathed it to the
State in 1881.

During his residence in Florence, Raphael frequently
visited his old master Perugino who had become rich and had
married a very beautiful young woman. It is told of
Perugino that he so admired a certain style of head dress
worn by his wife that he often arranged it himself, a story
which no doubt confirmed Michael Angelo's opinion that
Perugino "was no better than a blockhead." On one of these
visits to his old master and his young and charming wife at
Perugia, Raphael agreed to paint a picture of the *Entombment of Christ,* now in the Borghese Gallery in Rome. The
painting is six feet square and was the most considerable and
ambitious thing he had thus far undertaken. He seems to
have had much difficulty in drawing his original sketch as
is revealed in the numerous designs still in existence, in all
of which the Raphael feeling and the subtle delicacy of the
Raphael touch are everywhere present, though the subject
was not an appealing one to him. His clear and sunny spirit
delighted in scenes of joy, and was ill at ease when it perforce or otherwise became the bearer of unhappy messages.
He never painted a crucifixion after he was twenty. The
Entombment itself was painted as the result of a special
commission, the circumstances of which are sufficiently interesting to record.

Perugia, during the fifteenth and sixteenth centuries

was one of the most lawless cities of Italy, and while Raphael was studying there under Perugino it was the scene of one of the most frightful massacres in the annals of the land. The Baglione faction consisted of two brothers, Guido and Giovanni Paulo, and their children, and one sister Atalanta and her son Grifone. This Grifone for some reason became enraged at his uncles and only waited an opportunity to wreak vengeance upon them, an opportunity which came on the occasion of the marriage of his cousin Astone, son of Guido. The wedding ceremonies were celebrated with more than regal magnificence. A triumphal arch was raised in the city square adorned with banners proclaiming the brave deeds of the bridegroom, while a canopy was stretched over the entire square to protect the brilliant procession from rain. There were passages at arms and feasting and revelry which continued late into the night, the guests dispersing, most of them, under the influence of wine. Now had come the opportune moment for Grifone's vengeance, and he and his companions burst upon their sleeping victims. His uncle Guido fell first, then Astone, his wife vainly endeavoring to shield him with her own body from the assassins' daggers. When the deed was done, Grifone went to his mother and wife— they knew nothing about it—and asked their forgiveness, both of whom refused to listen and drove him away with curses. He returned to Perugia only to be in turn murdered by the followers of Giovanni Paulo, his surviving uncle. Hearing the sound of arms Atalanta, Grifone's mother, who had given him her curse and had never forgiven him, her mind presaging evil, ran into the street and among the dead and injured found Grifone dying of many wounds. It was this Atalanta Baglione who had Raphael paint his *Entombment* to commemorate the death of her son. Raphael, who had witnessed these lawless deeds, embodied them not only in the *Entombment* but in the *Heliodorus* and other great pictures he afterward painted in the Vatican. The *Entomb-ment* is a wail of despair in art, but it is not like Raphael, and he seemed to realize it, for he never painted another.

He was now twenty-five and the climax of his career was at hand. His fame had already reached Pope Julius, who summoned him to Rome. Julius had planned the decorations of the Vatican with care and a consummate knowledge of the fitness of the various artists whom he selected to do the work. The monumental frescoes of the Sistine Chapel were reserved for the genius of Michael Angelo, the other apartments he gave to Raphael. Angelo, always claiming to be a sculptor rather than a painter, insisted that Raphael be given his place but, fortunately for the world and for the fame of Michael himself, the Pope would not consent. That Raphael would have filled the Sistine vault with creations of surpassing beauty is not to be doubted, not for a moment, but that the sublime figures which are there could ever have been equalled in their own way by any other were an utter impossibility. Moreover, Raphael found ample scope for his genius where Pope Julius employed him.

His first work in the Vatican was done in the Camera della Segnatura, where he painted four pictures which would have immortalized any artist and which in their own way are as supreme as the Sistine frescoes are in theirs. These four pictures are the *Disputa,* the *School of Athens,* the *Parnassus* and the *Jurisprudence,* four magnificent productions in which the influence of a new motive is revealed. The secret of his power is no longer either Perugino or Leonardo exclusively, but a classical inspiration drawn from the superb Greek sculptures in the Vatican. From now on Raphael was more Greek than either Tuscan or Umbrian. There is much truth in what some critics say that he has Hellenized our conceptions of the Bible and painted Jehovah with the lineaments of Jupiter. Ruskin says that the doom of Christian art was sounded in the Camera della Segnatura. However all this may be, the pictures themselves are the most surpassingly beautiful representations of the kind in existence. Crowe and Cavalcaselle do not exaggerate when they say that "the *School of Athens* is simply the finest, best balanced and most perfect arrangement of figures that was ever put together by the genius of the Italian revival, and the scene in which the action is set is the most splendid display of monumental architecture that was ever made in the Sixteenth Century."

The plan of these four paintings was indeed superb. They were to represent the sum of knowledge through which man attains to the Universal Truth of Divinity. The four grand divisions of knowledge—Theology, Poetry, Philosophy and Jurisprudence (Raphael lived before the days of real science)—are represented by the four pictures, the *Disputa,* or dispute over the sacrament, the *Parnassus,* the *School of Athens* and the *Jurisprudence.* From the standpoint of art it is difficult to say which of these pictures is the greatest, though the *School of Athens,* representing Philosophy, is best known. The temptation scene in the *Disputa* is a striking example of the difference between Raphael and his great compeer, Michael Angelo, in the Sistine Chapel. In Angelo's picture Eve is a strong, vigorous woman with dark hair and passionate eyes who takes the "apple" boldly, while Adam is in such a hurry to get it that he plucks it himself. In Raphael's picture, on the contrary, Eve has golden hair, the gentlest expression on her face and a look of inquiring curiosity as she offers the "apple" to Adam. She is such a gentle creature that we can hardly see how she can sin.

The *School of Athens* is almost a text-book on Greek philosophy and reveals a remarkable knowledge of the subject on the part of the painter. Plato and Aristotle are in the centre of the picture, the former pointing upward to the heavens as a symbol of the idealistic tendencies of his system, while Aristotle significantly holds out his hands over the earth, thus indicating his scientific tendencies. Socrates is talking to the beautiful youth, Alcibiades, and the gestures of his hands indicate his skill in argument and in asking questions. Diogenes also has a prominent place in the middle of the stairs, having just crawled out of his tub in such a way that no one can come between him and the sun. Epicurus walks up the stairs keeping his back turned to Diogenes, the nobility of his figure symbolizing the superior type of the ethics of pleasure which he represents. These are but a very few of the figures, as this picture is a study in itself. To reflect that, in this painting alone, there are over fifty characters all thus clearly individualized, that they are all arranged in one harmonious plan, comprising a perfect unity, that the architectural setting is of a piece with all the rest helps us to understand what is meant when Raphael is styled the Shakspere of Art. It is their marvelous universality which links the dramatist and artist together and makes each of them supreme in his own respective field.

While working on the sketch for the *Disputa* Raphael seems to have written some very ardent sonnets which have been discovered on the back of the sketch. It is not known to whom they were addressed. Tradition says that the lady's name was Margherita and that Raphael fell in love with her when he saw her "feet twinkling" in the water of a fountain in her garden—much like the story of Robert of Normandy and Arletta, told by Palgrave and paraphrased by Creasy as follows:

"Arletta's pretty feet twinkling in the brook made her the mother of William the Conqueror. Had she not thus fascinated Duke Robert, the Liberal of Normandy, Harold would not have fallen at Hastings, no Anglo-Norman dynasty would have arisen, no British empire."

There are three pictures each of which has been called the Sweetheart of Raphael, one a dark-eyed girl in the Barberini Gallery at Rome, another a girl of a similar type in the Pitti Gallery at Florence and a third, also in the Pitti, called *La Donna Velata* because she wears a veil. The latter picture hangs by del Sarto's portrait of his beautiful wife, Lucrezia. The *Donna Velata* is a handsome woman with a deep, spiritual expression and features, strikingly like those of the Sistine Madonna. The other "sweethearts" of Raphael have been both called la Fornarina, because it was believed that the original of the pictures was a baker's daughter. The best authorities now, however, consider them apocryphal. There are no end of traditions about Raphael's love affairs, none of which has a very solid foundation in fact. His sonnets, which are bad poetry, some of his letters, which have been preserved, and the general testimony of contemporary writers indicate that he loved some woman all of his life, but who she was no one knows. It is certain, however, that Raphael, like Leonardo, Botticelli and Angelo, never married.

Besides the frescoes in the della Segnatura Raphael also, by special request of Pope Julius, painted four in the room of Heliodorus next to it, which, though masterly productions, hardly equal the others. These four are the *Expulsion of Heliodorus,* where a divine messenger visits him while he is stealing money from the treasury of the temple, as related in the *Second Book of the Maccabees,* the *Mass of Bolsena,* where the truth of transubstantiation was confirmed by a miracle, the *Deliverance of St. Peter from Prison* and the *Defeat of Attila* by the appearance in the sky of St. Peter and St. Paul. A very striking feature about the *Heliodorus* is the anachronism of Pope Julius enthroned in

The Donna Velata   *Florence*

By Raphael

7524

full canonicals, though the event that the picture represents took place in a Jewish temple over three hundred years before Christ. But Pope Julius always had an eye to the main chance. He wanted to connect these pictures with the needs of his own time, and saw no better way to do it than to have himself in the picture as if he were the directing and controlling power. The fate of Heliodorus was to teach people what would come of robbing or neglecting the Lord's (or the Pope's) treasury; the *Mass of Bolsena* was to be a lesson against heretical doctrines concerning the Real Presence in the Sacrament; the *Deliverance of St. Peter* was to emphasize the supremacy of that apostle in affairs of the church, and the *Defeat of Attila* was to be a warning to the modern barbarians of the North to keep their hands off of Italy. Pope Julius died after the first two frescoes were finished and Leo X., his successor, had the remaining two completed. Raphael's original plan was carried out with the exception that Leo insisted on having himself made immortal as Julius before him had done. It is easy to see the difficulties with which a painter in those times had to contend, when those in authority insisted on being placed in every picture he painted whether they fitted in or not. It must have been very exasperating to an artist, even to the point of desperation, when he was painting Apollo on Mount Parnassus to be confronted by an octogenarian with long beard and hooked nose who almost, if not altogether, demanded to have his features immortalized along with those of Apollo or Ganymede, the ideals of masculine grace and beauty. One artist, Michael Angelo, was not often molested in this way; he defied even Pope Julius, fiery as he was, driving him out on one occasion with a board for interfering with his work, pretending, of course, that he thought it was some one else; when he did put a distinguished person in a picture he put him in hell or in its environs; consequently, those in authority and others let him alone to paint as his own genius directed.

Pope Julius was a very remarkable man in every way. He was stern, high-tempered and warlike but withal upright, capable and honest. Asking Michael Angelo one day when he would complete his frescoes in the Sistine and the stern Michael gruffly replying "When I can," Julius hit the artist on the head with his cane, and afterward gave him five hundred ducats to heal the wound. When the old Pope went to the north to take command of his army against the French he felt so confident of immediate victory that he made a vow not to shave until the French were driven out of Italy. Though through all his previous life he had never worn a beard, he was, by virtue of his vow, destined to wear one during the remainder of his career, and in all the pictures after this, including the one of Heliodorus, he is shown with a long and ample beard. Raphael painted a very famous portrait of Pope Julius, the original of which appears to have been destroyed. There are three copies of this picture, one in the Uffizi Gallery, one in the Pitti and one in the National Gallery in London. The one in the Uffizi is catalogued as an original and Parsavant claims originality for the Pitti copy. The portrait in the Uffizi, whether original or not, is one of the greatest pictures ever painted and deserves all the fame it has achieved.

Pope Leo X., the successor of Julius, was a different type of man. He was a Medici and a pronounced Humanist, and with him Raphael's Greek tendencies were encouraged and allowed full play. In the famous portrait of Leo, now at Florence, he has a sensual though less cruel and more intellectual face than his successor Giuliano, the future Clement VII., painted in the same picture with him. We are told that this picture was so lifelike that Baldassare Turini, president of the chancery, took it for the reality and,

Portrait of Pope Julius II   *Florence*

By Raphael

kneeling before it, offered the pontiff a pen to sign some bills, a story which calls to mind that of Zeuxis' painting grapes so perfectly that it deceived the birds which tried to eat them and of Parrhasius' painting a veil so closely resembling the original that his competitor tried to remove it from the picture. These are the stories told of the contest between these two Greek painters.

Raphael's later work in the Vatican comprises the cartoons for the tapestries of the Sistine Chapel, the frescoes of the *loggie* or open galleries and the frescoes of the *stanza* of the Incendio del Borgo. As in the case of the Segnatura and Heliodorus there are also four in this room of del Borgo, all of them painted to glorify the spiritual ancestors of the reigning Pope Leo X. The first picture is the *Justification of Leo III.,* the second, the *Coronation of Charlemagne* by the same Leo, both pictures symbolizing the supremacy of the spiritual over the temporal power, the third, *Leo IV. Conquering the Saracens at Ostia* and the fourth, the *Miracle of Pope Leo IV.* in stopping the conflagration of the Borgo by making the sign of the cross. The powers of characterization, dramatic skill and subtlety of illustration displayed in this last picture are superb and make it one of Raphael's greatest works. It is in bad condition, though many attempts have been made to restore it to its original glory, the first by the Venetian painter, Sebastian del Piombo, of whom it is related that one day shortly after having, as he thought, improved it, he took his friend Titian to see it, who immediately on entering the room turned to the complacent Piombo with a disgusted look and said: "Who is the arrogant and ignorant man who has dared thus to daub over these heads?" Piombo stammered something about Giulio Romano, and at once began talking of something else.

Raphael planned a fourth *stanza,* the Constantine, which contains the famous *Battle of Constantine,* the largest

battle fresco in the world. The design is his but the work
was done by Giulio Romano. The other pictures are scenes
from the life of Constantine. The Segnatura *stanza* containing the *Disputa,* the *Parnassus,* the *School of Athens* and
the *Jurisprudence,* the Heliodorus *stanza* containing the
Expulsion of Heliodorus, the *Mass of Bolsena,* the *Defeat
of Attila* and the *Liberation of St. Peter,* the Incendio del
Borgo *stanza* containing the four scenes from the lives of
Popes Leo III. and IV., including particularly the burning
of the Borgo and the four episodes from the life of the
Roman Emperor Constantine, painted by his assistants,
chiefly Romano, constitute the four Raphael *Stanze* of the
Vatican.

The Raphael cartoons for the Sistine Chapel are almost
equally famous. They were designed for tapestries to hang
along the walls of the Sistine just underneath the side wall
frescoes. These tapestries, after many vicissitudes, with the
exception of two which were destroyed, are now in the Vatican, but the cartoons are in South Kensington Museum,
London, and are the most valuable of Raphael's work in the
possession of the English people. As a painter of religious
subjects, Raphael is at his best in these cartoons, principally
scenes from the life of Paul, and no work of his is any better
in technique. His Christ face, though incontestably a masterpiece, does not, in my judgment, equal Leonardo's in the
Last Supper.

After the stanze and the cartoons there remains the
work of Raphael for the popes in the *loggie* or open galleries
facing the inner court of the Vatican. The *loggie* are usually
called Raphael's Bible for they contain forty-eight scenes
from Biblical history, all beautifully done, though the conception of character and attitude is mostly Greek rather than
Hebrew. Beauty is beauty, whether historically accurate or

not, and Raphael clothed his religion in the fairest forms he knew.

Aside from his later work in the Vatican, Raphael painted for the Farnesina Palace his superb fresco of the *Galatea* and the *Legend of Cupid and Psyche*. Here is a Greek theme treated in a Greek manner and the result is exquisite harmony and beauty. To attempt to describe the delicacy of the *Galatea* is little short of sacrilege. If I had one hour to spend in Rome, outside the Vatican, I would go to the Farnesina. We must pass over his sibyls and prophets and must now turn to the great oil paintings of his later years, of which we can mention only four, the *St. Cecilia* at Bologna, the *Madonna della Sedia* at Florence, the *Sistine Madonna* at Dresden and the *Transfiguration* in the Vatican at Rome.

The *St. Cecilia* was painted under somewhat peculiar circumstances for Cardinal Pucci, whose musical talent was notoriously defective. His rebellious voice never sounded a note that did not jar on the whole college of cardinals. "When I began to sing," was his lament, "the prelates of the Sistine Chapel burst into irrepressible laughter." In vain did he refuse to officiate because he sang so wretchedly, and in his despair pleaded for the heavenly intercession of St. Cecilia, who inspired a master of the Sistine Chapel to come to his rescue, this man curing the cardinal's defects in six months. Doubtless Cardinal Pucci, like Artemus Ward, was saddest when he sang and those who heard him sadder still, or, as it appears, they recognized its incongruity, its comic aspects, and laughed instead.

The *Madonna della Sedia* in the Pitti Gallery is the most widely known and most popular Madonna in the world. Nearly every home has a copy of this picture with its chubby, over-sized Christ child and its mother, in her seemingly too narrow place, bending over it. I have seen copies of this

Madonna in homes where literature was confined to an almanac and a Bible. The original painting hangs opposite the *Granduca*. Its coloring is superb, among the best of Raphael's, though there are faults in the drawing. Its expression of simple mother love, with nothing beyond, has never been surpassed. It is a picture which the mothers of every nation and religion will always adore, and in its appeal to that deepest of all feelings lies the secret of its almost world-wide popularity. It is not, strictly speaking, a religious picture, differing widely in this respect from the *Granduca* and the *Sistine,* the latter of which is Raphael's greatest picture as well as his greatest Madonna.

As a work of art the *Sistine Madonna* surpasses the *Transfiguration,* while as a sublime inspiration it ranks with such creations as *Hamlet* and the *Divine Comedy,* creations which, to quote Horace, "strike the stars." The *Sistine Madonna* is a great poem, a movement of some divine symphony caught and fixed on canvas; it is the union of what is sweetest in humanity with what is most adorable in divinity, a picture of the fairest, truest affection of which a human soul is conscious. It should be kept in mind that the face of the *Sistine Madonna* is not an imaginary one but the features of a real woman, the same face as that of the *Donna Velata* in the Pitti Gallery. Raphael here, as everywhere else, painted a great Madonna because he loved a woman whose face was worthy of such an idealization.

But the end of the great artist was at hand. "Whom the gods love die young" has been exemplified many times in the history of literature and art. The close and constant application to such a tremendous volume of work as his, comprising over two hundred known pictures, so exhausted his physical strength that when he was stricken with fever on March 28, 1520, he lived only eight days. All Rome mourned his death, and the unfinished *Transfiguration* was exhibited above his bier. "Nothing," says a writer of the period, "is spoken of here but the death of this excellent man, who closed his first life at thirty-seven but the second, which is that of renown, is subject to neither time nor place and will be perpetual." Of his last great painting, the *Transfiguration,* it need only be said that it is worthy of Raphael. It is not as great as the *Sistine Madonna,* but the difficulties of composition were more serious, and then the painting is not entirely from the master's hand.

We have likened Raphael to Shakspere for obvious and sundry reasons. No other dramatist has produced so many excellent plays as Shakspere, neither has any other painter produced so many excellent paintings as Raphael. We may criticize him for this or that fault, as the critics have attacked Shakspere for disregarding the unities, but after all has been said, Raphael, like Shakspere, is still as great as ever. There are many things in the nature of each man's work which suggest the other, the most important of which, perhaps, is the marvelous objective power each one possessed. Shakspere varies his characters infinitely and is impartial toward all; likewise Raphael creates many kinds of faces, each one individualized and having a place to itself. Another very striking feature is the manner in which both borrowed and assimilated the teachings of their masters. Shakspere copied and digested Marlowe, Lyly and Kyd, Raphael did likewise with Perugino, Leonardo, and others, each doing this, it should always be kept in mind, without becoming a copyist or without surrendering any of his own individuality, the personal equation always being the supreme factor with both painter and dramatist. Another feature common to both is their religious and moral sanity. Both are normal in religion and morals. The works of both teach great moral lessons and emphasize great moral laws. Both show a decided preference for female characters. Raphael has painted a

great many more women than men and Shakspere has a
half dozen heroines for every hero. Both worked indefati-
gably, rapidly, both were more or less careless in matters of
detail. Shakspere was the most popular, most genial, most
kindly member of the Elizabethan School in London,
Raphael, as we have seen, held the same place with his fellow
artists in Rome. Many more points of similarity might be
noticed, but these will suffice.

Raphael's supreme greatness consists in his appeal to
what is highest and best in our ordinary human life. He
spoke a language that can be understood by all and painted
faces that all can love. His ultimate appeal is to the mother
feeling, the strongest impulse to which an appeal can be made.
He was not a philosopher like Leonardo and never touched
the depths of the *Mona Lisa,* but to most people the *Sistine
Madonna* means more, and always will, than Leonardo's masterpiece of personality. The problems of the world-wearied,
love-stricken Botticelli never touched the happy, light-
hearted Raphael, while Michael Angelo's masculine bias he
respected without especially admiring. As Leonardo pictured thought incarnate in a human face, so Raphael pictured incarnate love; and wherever love is found, wherever
a mother presses a child to her breast, wherever a human
heart throbs with unspeakable yearning for human affection,
there Raphael will be likewise loved and remembered and
honored.

ANDREA DEL SARTO

· · · · ·

The Tragedy of Genius

ANDREA DEL SARTO

One of the most popular churches in the city of Florence is the cloister of the Annunziata. Here the people gather in crowds to worship and not simply to enjoy the works of art for which so many of the churches in the city are distinguished. The Annunziata, while it cannot rival Santa Croce, Santa Maria Novella, San Lorenzo, San Marco or the Duomo, possesses art treasures of superior charm.

Perhaps the most famous fresco in the building is a lunette painted about four centuries ago. The drawing is still faultless and the colors, although faded, are better preserved than is usual in a painting four hundred years old. There are three figures in the small half-moon shaped picture, the traditional holy family group. The aged Joseph reclines upon a bag of grain reading a book, while Mary sits erect in the centre with her child on the right. This arrangement is simple, but in accordance with the best standards of art, the coloring, though subdued, harmonious and revealing a master's touch, the drawing faultless and so skilfully executed that it attracts the attention of even those who know nothing of the technique of painting. Even the most Philistine admirer of art must recognize that he is in the presence of a masterpiece.

The Madonna is, of course, the central figure. She is very beautiful in face and form with the roses of eternal youth upon her lips, but when we look beneath the physical charm to discover what her thoughts are we are disappointed. In her soulless eyes there is no expression of very deep affection for her child, no touch of that mother love which beams from every line of Raphael, none of the anxiety and sad, but

profound, questioning of Botticelli, and, above all, no
approach to those depths of thought, to that far-seeing wisdom, to that revelation of the infinite, written in the face
and eyes of Mona Lisa. What is there in that face of perfect
physical beauty? Eve or Venus was not more faultless.
But withal this there is something lacking, something—the
most important of all—that ought to be there but is not.
"What is wrong with her face?" I once asked a student who
was looking at the picture. After a moment she replied: "I
don't know, only it doesn't seem to have any soul." This was
a just criticism—the woman does not have any soul. She is
not worried over her child because neither her child, nor
anything else, can disturb her. She is conscious of her
physical charms, thinks of them perhaps with a little womanly pride, though evidently not much disturbed about them.
She feels neither love nor hatred, anxiety nor care. And it
is all because she has no soul. Notwithstanding this fatal
defect, the picture is very beautiful and will always attract
any who admire perfection in drawing or color. There is
too much drapery, but how artistically arranged! Her hands
are exquisite. Mona Lisa's hands are not so lovely nor her
face so beautiful. Mona Lisa!—We start at the words, we
are universes distant from her; and yet, if del Sarto's
Madonna had but a little only of which Mona Lisa has so
much, what a transcendently glorious creation she would be!
An Aphrodite, a Pallas Athene, a Helen of Troy, the original Platonic archetype of woman, perfection of body and
perfection of soul—if she had only had a soul—what a pity
she could not have existed, at least, on canvas! On a pillar
next to the man in the picture are the Latin words "quem
genuit adoravit" and on another pillar the words "Anno
Domini 1525." In the meantime your guide has been telling
you in weird Tuscan of a certain lady, whose name he does
not know, who had committed a grievous sin which ate out

her heart, leaving her no peace day or night. At last she
learns what she may do to expiate her sin and find peace
for her soul. She can have a lunette painted for the new
church of the Annunziata, and inquiring for the best painter
in Florence she is told to go to Andrea Agnolo, popularly
known as Andrea del Sarto. "And so, Signore," the guide
continues, "the picture was painted. It is very beautiful,
as you see. But would you like to go on to the next?"

We have been looking at and contemplating the
Madonna del Sacco, which, though in bad condition, is still
one of the most beautiful of all the paintings of Andrea del
Sarto. In the same church, near the high altar, rests the
body of him who painted the physically beautiful but soulless
Madonna. It was a cold January evening in the year 1530
when the body of this genius who could have rivaled Raphael
was borne to the tomb in the church of the Annunziata, unat-
tended by relatives or friends. His mother and father were
dead, and his wife, whom he had immortalized on so many
canvases, had callously deserted him while he lay dying of
the plague. Only a few barefooted friars of the Scalzo,
who had remained true to the last, were present to perform
the final rites and arrange for a few masses for the soul
of the dead artist. There is an entry in the books of the company of St. Sebastian to the effect that on January 23, 1530,
an office was said for the soul of Andrea del Sarto, whom it
had pleased God to remove *al suo beato regno* ("to his blessed
kingdom"). What a contrast with that of another funeral
scene at Rome less than ten years before, when, after lying
in state for several days with his last great masterpiece
hanging above him, the body of the painter of the *Transfiguration* was borne, accompanied by a vast concourse of
people of all classes, from St. Peters to the Pantheon where
it was interred with all the glory and magnificence of which
such a church is capable. And yet Raphael never drew a

figure as perfect as many of del Sarto's, and as a colorist
was a mere amateur beside him.   What a little difference
there is, after all, between success and failure, as the world
estimates them!   But for Lucrezia del Fede, there might
have been another and a greater tomb than Raphael's in the
Pantheon, because of better pictures in the Vatican.   But we
are anticipating.

Andrea del Sarto lived five years longer than Raphael
and less than half as long as Michael Angelo, dying at the
age of forty-two.   During his career as an artist he painted
over two hundred pictures, not one of which may be called
bad, though, of course, some are much better than others.
The date of his birth is uncertain, most of the evidence
being in favor of the year 1488.   He was the third of six
children, his father being a tailor, as the name indicates.   His
ancestors came originally from Ghent, whence his grand-
father had to flee because in a fit of anger he had killed a
man with whom he had quarreled over the misfit of a coat.
This tailor from Ghent settled in Florence, where some years
later Andrea del Sarto was born.   At the age of seven
Andrea's father placed him with a goldsmith, where he displayed such a decided skill in drawing that the elder Agnolo
put him under the tutelage of Piero di Cosimo, one of the
best artists in Florence, and as eccentric in the world of
painting as Dean Swift was in the world of letters.   Piero
took special delight in painting all sorts of mythological
scenes with fantastic settings.   He was never married, lived
alone, prepared his own meals, and, toward the last, never
allowed his room to be swept or his garden cultivated.   He
would boil as many as fifty eggs at a time and eat them at
intervals when he was hungry.   The ringing of bells, the
sound of voices, even the flies on the wall, gave him severe
nervous suffering.   He permitted no one about him, and was
found dead one morning at the bottom of the stairs.

Andrea remained with di Cosimo until the latter's eccentricities made life unbearable, when, with a young friend named Franciabigio, to whom he was devotedly attached, he left Cosimo. Both of the young men were good artists and soon had all the work they could do. One of the first contracts they accepted was for the Brotherhood of the Scalzo, or Barefooted Friars, as they were called, who were bound by vows to the strictest poverty and humility, and whose patron saint was St. John the Baptist, the special guardian of Florence. They frescoed, in the most subdued coloring, the walls of the cloister of the Scalzo with twelve scenes from the life of St. John. For the large pictures the artists were to receive fifty-six lire, or about eleven dollars each, and for the small ones twenty-two lire, a little more than four dollars each. These frescoes, which were not finished for many years, constitute some of del Sarto's greatest work, and few paintings in Italy are worth more careful study or are more interesting from the standpoint of art. Before completing these pictures he was asked to paint some frescoes in the church of the Annunziata, which are to-day scarcely less interesting than those of the Scalzo. For these immortal productions he received a little less than ten dollars for each one. He also painted many easel pictures during this period, by far the happiest of his life. A great future was before him, a future of fame and unbounded success, so those who knew his ability predicted.

Going to and from his work in the Scalzo cloister, Andrea went along the Via di San Gallo, which is the next street running parallel with that now called the Via Cavour, the street on which the Scalzo church is located. Every day he passed by the house of a cap maker named Carlo Recanati. It was not long before he found out that a very pretty woman lived in the Recanati house, and one apparently not altogether indifferent to his presence. It is a story the like of which has been told since consciousness began. Every time Andrea saw the fair Lucrezia he thought her more beautiful and charming. Were there ever such exquisite hands or such perfect features as hers, or hair of such golden abundance? What treasures for a lover of beauty like himself! what glories! The lines of her face came before him and the dry fresco on the wall of the Scalzo, and he half-unconsciously painted it just as it appeared in his vision. She came to look at his work and was proud of it, proud that so brilliant a man, so romantic an artist was her lover. Perhaps in those days she loved him a little, as much as she could love anything, but her love was at all times very different from his.

Inspired by her, he worked so assiduously that in one year, 1514, he finished three of the series—the *Birth of St. John,* the *Preaching of the Baptist,* and the *Baptism of the Multitude.* In the second of these frescoes Lucrezia appears among the attendants who crowd around listening to the words of the Prophet. The appeal, "Repent, for the Kingdom of Heaven is at hand," produces feelings of different kinds upon those who hear. There are the proud Pharisees, who smile contemptuously, and the bold soldier, rough in appearance, who expresses in his face that the words of the Prophet have touched him deeply; there are also penitents, who believe without question what the speaker says; there are others half-incredulously wondering whether any of it is true or not. Among them all, Lucrezia sits alone. Her marvelously beautiful face betrays not a touch of emotion or feeling, and the question, "What is she doing there?" rises involuntarily to our lips, only to be stilled in the realization that she was put there by an inward compulsion which the artist could not escape. As certain saints and figures were put in pictures of other artists by direct command of those in authority, whether in keeping or not, so Andrea paints the face of Lucrezia in nearly every picture, which it seemed he could not finish without painting her once, at least. In most of his pictures she is the central figure, in all (except where it was impossible) she appears in some guise or other. This is not imaginary, neither is it exaggerated; it is plain, unvarnished fact.

It is noteworthy also that in this continual portraiture of Lucrezia, the artist has shown the utmost delicacy and care in selecting the place in the picture which he reserved for her. Other painters, not excepting Botticelli or Raphael, most of all, Titian and Rubens, have used their sweethearts and wives as models for Venuses and Floras and other beautiful creations sanctioned by art, but not always by the innate modesty of genuine affection. Whether intended or not these painters, for the sake of its artistic value, have sacrificed the mysteries and intimacies of love, carelessly, indifferently revealing the hidden arcana of what ought to be kept inviolably and sacredly veiled, and have sold their richest treasures for the glittering bauble of artistic fame. But not so with Andrea, who loved too deeply, if not wisely, for this. Whatever Lucrezia might be to others and whatever others might think of her, to him she remained always sacred. As Charity, the highest of the Christian graces, as one of those who followed John the Baptist, the forerunner of Christ, as the Divine Mother herself, always, everywhere, she is given the place of honor, and there is never the slightest suggestion about her position or attitude or drapery which would cause the remotest criticism from the most evil-minded person who looks at her picture. What a terrible tragedy that the object of such chivalrous homage, all too rare in any time or country, should have been so little worthy of it! It is not necessary to accept Vasari's statements concerning the soulless character of Lucrezia; her features, faultlessly portrayed by her lover and husband, tell the story better than words.

Lucrezia's illiterate husband died in 1516 and she mar-

ried Andrea soon after.   His family and friends very bitterly opposed the union, but their objections were lost sight
of in the storm of his affection, a storm, by the way, which
never quite spent all its fury.   She never forgot or forgave
their opposition and made them pay for it afterward with
tears of anguish.   Andrea had always helped to care for his
parents and other members of his family; now, by Lucrezia's
mandate, he must give them up.   She threatened him, if he
refused, with the loss of her own love.   To one so gentle and
kind-hearted as Andrea is known to have been, it must have
been a crushing blow.   There was no doubt as to what he
would do.   Was there anything too high or holy to sacrifice
for her?   Indeed, was not his whole life one long and continual crucifixion for this beautiful, soulless woman?   He
gave up his aged father who had loved him and had made his
career possible, and his mother who had been proud of him
and had refused him nothing; never any more did he go to
their home, as had been his custom, something for which
he was hated by his brothers and despised by his friends.
How these things must have weighed upon Andrea's sensi-
tive soul, and how it must have robbed his art of the glory
it might have won!   Though his course was wrong, he could
not do otherwise; he loved his wife, strangely, blindly, madly,
unwisely, hopelessly; fate loaded the dice against him when
he allowed his eyes to wander to her window in the Via di
San Gallo and his thoughts to linger with her in the cloisters
of the Scalzo.   He loved her; that was all; that settled all.
Brothers might hate and friends despise and others blame,
but to him it made no difference so far as his actions were
concerned.   With the loss of friends his profession became
less remunerative, and the demands of his wife, who cared
for nothing but the adornment of her body, more insistent
and oppressive.   Instead of caring for his own family she had
him take care of hers.   Her cousins and relatives must be

provided for, and she expected him to do it. Never having really loved him, she soon gave him some cause, though perhaps but little, for jealousy. Of all his afflictions, this was the most bitter; so long as he retained her, he could stand the loss of everything else; but once lose her, all had gone, the bitterness of the loss of all the others being accentuated in this, his greatest misfortune. It does not appear that Lucrezia treated him unkindly, indeed, throughout her life she loved him as much as it was possible for her to love anyone, but for her to appreciate or return, even in the smallest measure, his love and affection, was impossible.

Things dragged on in this way, Andrea getting deeper and deeper in debt and Lucrezia constantly demanding money that he did not have. Then one day, just two years after their marriage, there was a rift in their financial clouds. A few years previously, Puccini, a Florentine merchant, had sent Andrea's picture of the *Dead Christ Mourned by Angels* to France, where it was sold for a high price. This picture, coming eventually to the notice of Francis the First, the most knightly of all the rulers of Christendom, so pleased the king that he at once gave orders for another. Andrea soon did a Madonna of extraordinary beauty, according to Vasari, and which is believed to be one of the pictures of the Holy Family now in the Louvre. This picture so delighted Francis that he could not sufficiently praise it, for all the paintings that his agents had brought from Italy, none approached that of Andrea. The king believed that with del Sarto at his court he could rival the work of Raphael and Michael, who were in Rome adorning the Vatican.

Meanwhile, things were growing worse with the luckless Andrea at home. He worked hard, painting among other pictures his *St. Sebastine,* which contains perhaps the best Christ face he ever drew, and an altar piece for the Servite

monks. These pieces brought him very little money, and he
was in despair at being constantly compelled to refuse the
sums he would so willingly and gladly have lavished upon
Lucrezia. It was at this time that messengers from Francis
arrived at Florence offering Andrea inducements which
must have sounded like an El Dorado to the hapless painter.
As an earnest of their king's good will, they brought heaps
of glittering gold pieces, more than Andrea had ever seen
before in his life, to equip him for the journey to France and
to pay the expenses of the trip. Though the temptation was
great, how could he leave Lucrezia for months, perhaps
years? In those days the journey over the Alps was considerable, and Francis would not be satisfied with a short
period of service. Whether to leave Lucrezia, that he might
be able to pour into her lap the golden florins for which she
so hungered, or to remain with her, this was Andrea's problem; he cared for the money which his genius and skill could
make only that he might bestow it upon her. As for Lucrezia
she cared a great deal for money and not much for the unfortunate Andrea, and she settled the question of his going. A
few kind words from her, telling him how dearly she would
love him when he returned with riches and how happy their
lives would be in the nebulous future (the future is always
nebulous) when the burden of poverty was removed, decided
the question. And so Andrea, knight errant of love and art,
became a "diver in strange seas" seeking for pearls to adorn
the beautiful, soulless woman whom he adored. He would
paint as he had never yet painted, he would for once ear-
nestly try to achieve fame as well as money, he would become
the cynosure of all eyes and his Lucrezia would love him
more devotedly than she had ever done before. Was there
not another painter, only four years his senior, whose fame
filled the world, who was attended by a retinue like a prince
and who reigned supreme in both love and art? And yet had

not the great master, Michael Angelo, said that Andrea could draw better than Raphael, and did not he himself know that he excelled Raphael as a master of color? The fame for which he had never cared he now thirsted for, because it meant Lucrezia's love. Before he departed for France he made every possible arrangement for her comfort. He had a new house furnished for her near the church of the Annunziata, and with the money, Francis had gladly advanced, provided for all her wants. He signed a deed of acknowledgment giving bond for one hundred florins, his wife's dowry, which, in the event of his death, was to be paid to her. Most of his friends in Florence believed when he set out for France that he would not return. They believed that he would win great fame in Paris and remain there, as Raphael and Michael Angelo had stayed in Rome. So universal was this opinion that the Scalzo brotherhood gave the contract they had with him to his friend, Franciabigio.

When Andrea arrived in Paris, King Francis showered presents of money and rich vestments upon him, giving him at once commissions for any and all pictures he could paint. Here was his opportunity—and what a field was open to him! All past events in French history:—the glories of Charlemagne and Orlando, Charles Martel and St. Genevieve of Paris, and greater than all others, the Maid of Orleans, triumphant even in the fires of Rouen, foremost of all earth's heroines. What a field for his imagination!—But then there was the Lucrezia ideal—a travesty on Joan of Arc or Genevieve. Andrea, realizing that he could never escape the obsession of Lucrezia's beauty, soulless as it was, continued to paint Holy Families with her as the central figure and Charities in which she overshadowed everything else. These works were received with the highest praise, which they well deserved. With the light gone out and his ambition crushed, he did extraordinary work in view of the lessened enthusiasm which remained to him. In all of these pictures what superb drawing, delicacy of outline and mastery of technique are seen! The *Charity* is regarded, even now, as one of the greatest treasures of the Louvre, and one, we are safe in saying, that will never lose its charm.

King Francis was in ecstasies over the beautiful work of the painter and promised him about everything if he would continue. Doubtless he had noticed the anxious, haunted look on Andrea's face which told of his homesickness and discontent. To encourage the artist in his work the king came almost every day to see him. When Andrea painted the Dauphin, only two months old, the king gave him a purse containing more money than he had made in Florence during all his life there. The unhappy artist worked feverishly all day and dreamed of Lucrezia all night, but never thought of returning. Considering his handicap, he had done exceedingly well, but he had only started. Thus far he had painted only easel pictures, while frescoes were his forte. Raphael, Angelo and Leonardo had achieved immortality in fresco work, and he would do it too. He would fill Paris with pictures like those in the Sala of the Vatican, a thing not impossible for del Sarto to accomplish, allowing even for the Lucrezia obsession; in point of technique he was superior to any of the others, and was just in the prime of life. What he needed was the inspiration which was given him in the unstinted praise and encouragement of Francis, now his friend as well as patron. According to Vasari, he was "winning toward the goal" in the *St. Jerome* on which he was working when he received the fatal letter which changed everything. A *St. Jerome* meant something stronger than Andrea had attempted for many years. Could he give the haggard and emaciated hermit the expression which, as an artist, he knew was essential, he would, to say the least, be approaching Raphael and Angelo. For Andrea to equal

Raphael in the point of expression would be to surpass him, for the former was faultless in technique while the latter was far from being so.

But the letter from Lucrezia had come, and with it a long farewell to greatness and dreams of glory. She had never before written him such a loving and ardent letter. Her devotion had never been what he had always longed for it to be, and now, that he was absent, she was lavish in her words of love. She was so disconsolate, she so longed for him, weeping night and day, and without him she could not endure to live. What, thought Andrea, if she were to die because of his absence; he would hate the gold of Francis and the glory he might win. That her protestations of love might not be sincere never entered the mind of the devoted Andrea, who had crushed down his own heart that he might work more efficiently to win gold and fame for her. Few indeed there are among the children of men who take pains to disprove that which the heart wants to believe. He had come to Paris to win Lucrezia's love again, and that won, why stay longer? So he resolved to go back to her. It was no easy matter to get away from Francis, and he succeeded in doing so only on the pretext that he wanted to purchase other and still rarer works of art, which he alone could secure, for the adornment of the French capital. At last, the great King sorrowfully gave his consent for him to go, exacting a promise, confirmed by an oath upon the Gospels, that he would soon return. There can be no doubt that Andrea intended to return and had not the remotest thought of embezzling the money he took with him.

Lucrezia, beautiful as ever, her features as perfect, her hair as rich and abundant, her voice as soft and musical, was glad to see him, for, aside from everything else, he brought a fortune with him. Moreover, in his new French clothes, covered with gold and gems, the gifts of Francis, he was a very handsome husband of whom she might feel as proud as when she first knew him. Of one thing Andrea soon became cognizant, and that was her dreams of how to spend his money, for her plans entailed an expenditure which even kingly gifts could not meet. He thought of returning to France, but it was easier, if more dishonorable, to remain and appropriate the money entrusted to him for the purchase of pictures. As much as we should like not to believe this about Andrea, the fact remains, which Vasari's statement to the contrary has never disproved. Some have maintained that the financial records of Francis show no such loss, a fact which does not prove anything, for the king could have easily given him the money from his own private purse and have made no record of it. This is probable considering the friendly relations which existed between them. Before Andrea misappropriated the money, he tried in every way to induce Lucrezia to go to Paris, but in vain. She wanted to remain with her friends and relatives. They had a beautiful house in Florence—it is still there. The rooms are attractively frescoed and the oak balustrades of the very finest. The furniture and other appointments were in keeping with the rest. At any rate, Andrea did not return.

When Francis learned that the artist was not coming back he vowed vengeance upon the man whom he now regarded as a perjurer and a thief. Andrea, doubtless feeling the sting of dishonor, tried to patch it up by sending the king some new pictures. As the weak and love-lorn artist had given up his parents for Lucrezia, so he now sacrificed both honor and fame, surrendering the most brilliant opportunities for her.

His last great picture, the *Last Supper,* at San Salvi, was painted in 1526, just five years before his death. This painting, once seen, can never be forgotten; it is the only Last Supper that should be mentioned in comparison with Leonardo's. It is painted in the refectory of San Salvi, which is just outside the walls of Florence. When the latter city was besieged by the French, an order was issued to raze this convent, but when the soldiers entered the refectory and saw this superb painting they stopped short, and their commander told them to leave the building unharmed. I shall never forget the first time I saw this picture. It was raining, and I was the only and solitary visitor for the day. At the moment I entered the refectory the clouds cleared away allowing a few scattered rays of sunlight to shine into the room, and, like the French soldiers, I stood still when the picture burst in full splendor on my sight. The figures are strangely animated and the coloring good. There is only one thing it lacks—the face of Jesus is not the face of the Christ. Andrea was not equal to the task; if the great Leonardo was incapable of measuring up to such a responsibility —he always felt that he was—the lover of Lucrezia could not even approach it. Yet, with this defect, it is a great picture, and only by seeing it can del Sarto be understood and appreciated. It was his last great effort to achieve something better than he had done, and the pathetic tragedy of his Christ face tells the story of the wreck of his hopes. So often had Andrea painted Lucrezia as his central figure that he could imagine no other greater than she. Her beautiful, soulless face was his ideal, which ideal he had realized so often that it seemed he could not pass beyond it. In this connection I quote from Vasari:

"If at any time he took his model from any other face, there was a resemblance to her in the painting, not only because he had this woman constantly before him and depicted her so frequently, but also, and what is still more, because he had her lineaments engraven on his heart: it thus happens that almost all of his female heads have a certain something which recalls that of his wife."

Andrea could not escape or overpass his ideal. He never reached the heights, because he never hitched his wagon to a star. Ideals, unless they are lofty ones, narrow our horizons and shrink our powers to correspond with them. Milton tells how the rebel angels, once stately and majestic beings, shrank in size to fit their meaner place in Hell. The spirit of man never passes beyond the boundary line which his ideals mark out for him. What matters if there be infinitude around him everywhere, what matters if there be infinite reaches to be won, if his ideal is always within his grasp? Andrea's farthest reach, his uttermost boundary line of thinking and acting was the beautiful, soulless, thoughtless face of Lucrezia, beyond which he could not go in conception or execution. This ideal he painted perfectly, and could not develop farther because there was nothing beyond for him; therefore, he is sometimes called "the faultless painter." In Browning's great monologue on Andrea del Sarto, the artist says, speaking to Lucrezia:

> "I can do with my pencil what I know,
> What I see, what at bottom of my heart
> I wish for, if I ever wish so deep—
> Do easily, too—when I say, perfectly,
> I do not boast—'tis easy all of it!
> No sketches first, no studies, that's long past;
> I do what many dream of all their lives,
> —Dream? strive to do, and agonize to do,
> And fail in doing. All is silver-gray
> Placid and perfect with my art: the worse!
> Ah, but a man's reach should exceed his grasp,
> Or what's a heaven for?"

This lack of "reach" in Andrea, explains his failure, and his want of "reach" was the result of his absorption in the Lucrezia ideal, an ideal too commonplace and limiting for any great achievement, especially in characterization such as distinguished the work of Leonardo or Angelo.

Andrea and Lucrezia

By Andrea del Sarto

Florence

Andrea del Sarto was a perfect painter not only in his always reaching his limited ideal in the face of Lucrezia, but also in his comparatively perfect technique and execution. So perfect was his work that it deceived the eye even of painters themselves. As an illustration of this the following story is in point: The Duke of Mantua, having a great desire for Raphael's portrait of Leo the Tenth, which he saw one day as he was passing through Florence, begged it of Pope Clement, one of the prominent figures portrayed in the painting. The Pope consented and commanded Ottaviano de Medici, the reigning duke, to send it to Mantua. Ottaviano, realizing that it was necessary to obey the Pope's order and not wanting to give up Raphael's great picture, commissioned Andrea del Sarto to make him a copy of it. So perfect was Andrea's copy, that not only the Duke of Mantua was deceived, but Giulio Romano, who assisted Raphael in painting it, declared that he could even tell the marks of his own brush. Long after, the copy was sent to Naples, and was the cause of a lengthy dispute during the nineteenth century between Naples and Florence as to which had the original. This is an illustration of Andrea's perfect skill, and is sufficient evidence, I think, to warrant the statement, that had his ideal been as unlimited as his technique was perfect, he would have excelled Leonardo and Raphael, and would have indeed and in fact been the perfect painter. As it was, they, as he himself says, in Browning's monologue, reached

> "Many a time a heaven that's shut to me,
> Enter and take their place there sure enough,
> Though they come back and cannot tell the world."

But the life of this potentially supreme artist was approaching its end. One evening a year or two before he died, he called Lucrezia to him and, taking up a tile, asked her to sit for her portrait, telling her that he wanted the world to see how well she had preserved her beauty. A biographer, speaking of this event, says that "the woman would not remain still, perhaps because she had other things in her head at the same moment." Afterward, Andrea painted his own picture, now in the Uffizi Gallery, by the use of a mirror. His face has changed since the earlier portrait; it is less spiritual and the eyes seem glazed and dull. There is no light of inspiration or thought there. It was perhaps well for this tragedy of genius that the end was near. Andrea died of the plague which ravaged Florence, deserted by his wife, who, of course, would take no risk for the man who had loved her not wisely but too well. No more pathetic character ever lived than Andrea del Sarto. It is sheer folly to say what he ought to have done and what he should not have done—such observations are always fatuous. Had he done other than he did, he would have been another personality and not Andrea del Sarto. Another personality would not have loved Lucrezia del Fede as he loved her. It is always easier to say what ought to be done than it is to do it. "If to do were as easy as to know what were good to be done, chapels had been churches and poor men's cottages princes' palaces." In Browning's monologue, Andrea says: "How free we seem, how fettered fast we are!" It is equally fatuous to condemn Lucrezia. She had no soul, of course— there are thousands of women and men the world over just like her, only many of them worse. The soulless are always pitiable. It was a tragedy for Andrea del Sarto to marry Lucrezia del Fede; she was the fatal and, to him, irresistible attraction which proved stronger than his personality or genius, and in the end destroyed both. The tragedy was inescapable, once he came within the circle of her fatal attraction and the more fatal beauty which intrigued his soul. We do not apologize for either of the two characters; the entire situation is one of those fateful happenings in our human

Madonna of the Harpies   *Florence*

By Andrea del Sarto

life from which there seems to be no escape, and for which there is no adequate explanation.

In the room in the Pitti Gallery where the famous picture of Andrea and Lucrezia hangs, the painting which inspired Browning to write his poem, are also the pictures of the women loved by Raphael and Titian. Raphael's, which contains the same face as the *Sistine Madonna,* is filled with spirituality and depth, Titian's, a proud society queen, clad in costly furs and velvet, has considerable intelligence, despite her being emphatically an idealization of fleshly beauty; but Lucrezia's, with perfect features and beautiful hair, has no touch of inspiration or soul. We read in the faces of these women the history of the men who loved them.

Of the many works of Andrea on canvas, the *Madonna of the Harpies* in the Uffizi Gallery stands as easily the greatest, the *Charity* in the Louvre ranking next. In its way, there is nothing anywhere more exquisite than the first named painting. Raphael himself never drew a more bewitching child picture. Lucrezia, the mother, is here seen at her best, an unmatched beauty with a bit of soul. It may have been to this tiny bit of soul that Andrea clung and in which he never entirely lost faith.

Over forty-nine Holy Families are attributed to him, some of which are exquisitely beautiful, the best among them being in the Louvre, in the Dresden Gallery and in the Pitti Gallery. His large pictures of the Assumption in the Pitti have too much drapery, and Lucrezia her most soulless look. The *Abraham* at Dresden is a fine painting. Neither should the lovely *St. Agnes* at Pisa, or the splendid *Disputa* in the Pitti be forgotten, the latter of which is, in my opinion, his most skilfully planned work.

In fresco he has left three great series—the Scalzo, the Annunziata and the Salvi. The frescoes of the Scalzo are executed with a grace and delicacy which must be seen to be appreciated. No one can form a proper estimate of Andrea del Sarto without seeing the cloister of the Scalzo on the Via Cavour. One of the most marvelous things about the twelve pictures, all representing scenes in the life of John the Baptist, is the manner in which the artist complied with the requirement of the barefooted friars to paint only in colors and tints of the ground, and at the same time managed to get such a variety and delicacy of color. The Scalzo is well worth a pilgrimage to see.

Of Andrea del Sarto, as a painter, all has been said perhaps that needs to be written. In drawing he has not been excelled by any member of the Florentine school, not even by Michael Angelo, though the latter usually chose to draw more difficult subjects. The Venetians alone rival him in color. Aside from his lack of spirituality, already noticed, his greatest fault was his over use of draperies. While Michael Angelo emphasized the artistic power of the nude, Andrea clung to the graceful draperies, keeping in this way, if nothing else, his own individuality. To many of us the sweet, sad pictures, with their ineffable coloring and exquisite harmony, bring more delight and pleasure than even the tremendous epics on the Sistine ceiling. When everything has been said and all criticisms made, the fact remains, as a critic has observed, that "Andrea has the despotism of charm."

In the face and eyes of Mona Lisa Leonardo hid the mystery of personality; in his wistful, questioning faces Botticelli symbolized the discontent of the ideal in its struggle with the actual; in his tremendous masculine genii on the Sistine ceiling Michael Angelo glorified the strength and sublimity of power; in his Madonnas Raphael idealized incarnate love in motherhood; these in their own way are supreme. But of Andrea del Sarto, who confessed his life a failure,

The Assumption of the Virgin   By Andrea del Sarto

Florence

whose faces have no inspiration and teach no sublime lesson, what shall we say? Has he no message for us? Yes, a profound one. It is of such importance that Robert Browning wrote two great poems about it, and has alluded to it, directly or by implication, in nearly all of his major work. It is the kernel of Goethe's Faust, the incarnation of his Mephistopheles — the complete sinking of the ideal in the actual, the complete cessation of struggle for a higher goal, the satisfaction of the soul with its achievements, and its being contented to accept what has been won as final and complete. In other words, the ideal has been irretrievably lost in the actual.

Andrea's work was perfect of its kind, but the low standard of mere technical perfection which he set was not high enough to raise him above the earth to the divine completeness which was in Raphael and Leonardo. The Lucrezia influence too, as has been noticed, had its weight. He loved her so entirely that to him she stood for womanhood, as the woman a man loves best will always stand, and by lowering his ideal she made the heights impossible for him. Hamlet wondered how his mother could live with his father without appreciating him, and the student of Andrea wonders often why Lucrezia could not appreciate her husband. She never understood him at all. I do not blame him or her. That she could do otherwise were impossible, and to expect it of her were little short of madness.

It should always be remembered that there is something very noble about the love which is too strong to save its votary from ruin. Had Raphael loved Lucrezia and Andrea Margherita the one might have been less than Andrea and the other greater than Raphael. However all this, and all the rest, may be, the work of Andrea will live and the story of his love for Lucrezia will appeal to every heart that has really loved.

It's a great picture that Browning paints of Andrea
del Sarto in his splendid poem.   It is evening, and the
shadows are lengthening over Fiesole.   Andrea is alone.
Tumultuous thoughts fill his soul, angry recriminations rise
in his brain; he thinks of his father and mother forsaken, of
his failure, his ruin.   It grows dark.   The light fall of a
dainty foot is heard.   "O so light a foot shall ne'er wear
out the everlasting flint!"   The touch of a hand, such as no
Greek sculptor ever carved, is laid upon his fevered brow.
At the magic touch the anger passes, the tumultuous brain
is still.   To the frivolous and fair Lucrezia he pours out
what remains of his tired soul:

> "I often am much wearier than you think,
> This evening more than usual, and it seems
> As if—forgive now—should you let me sit
> Here by the window with your hand in mine
> And look a half-hour forth on Fiesole,
> Both of one mind, as married people use,
> Quietly, quietly, the evening through,
> I might get up to-morrow to my work
> Cheerful and fresh as ever.   Let us try.
> To-morrow, how you shall be glad for this!
> Your soft hand is a woman of itself.
>
> "You loved me quite enough, it seems to-night.
> This must suffice me here.   What would one have?
> In heaven, perhaps, new chances, one more chance—
> Four great walls in the New Jerusalem,
> Meted on each side by the angel's reed,
> For Leonard, Rafael, Agnolo and me
> To cover—the three first without a wife,
> While I have mine!   So—still they overcome
> Because there's still Lucrezia,—as I choose."

The Dispute Over the Trinity
By Andrea del Sarto

Florence

TITIAN

. . . .

Painter of Materialistic Culture

TITIAN

"I stood in Venice on the Bridge of Sighs;
A palace and a prison on each hand:
I saw from out the wave her structures rise
As from the stroke of an enchanter's wand:
A thousand years their cloudy wings expand
Around me, and a dying Glory smiles
O'er the far times when many a subject land
Look'd to the winged Lion's marble piles,
When Venice sate in state, throned on her hundred isles!"
—Byron's "Childe Harold."

There is an enchantment about the very name of Venice which the centuries cannot dispel. It is true that to-day very little of the ancient Queen of the Adriatic remains, and the city is scarcely more than a pleasure resort where wealthy Americans contribute to the support of a parasitic population. To those who know her past but never saw her before, Venice is at first sight a disappointment, and only a vivid imagination can reconstruct the city of Dandolo and Faliero, the once proud mistress of the sea "throned on her hundred isles, the revel of the earth, the masque of Italy." Still many of her former characteristics cling round her—her atmosphere of luxuriance, her lack of moral sentiment, her splendid charm of scenery and location, these are all there.

The Genius of Painting is as distinct in Venice from her sisters in Florence or Rome as the peoples are distinct in manners, customs and life. We differentiate Leonardo, Botticelli, Angelo, and Raphael; but after all they are as essentially alike as different branches of the same tree or different children of the same parents. But when we come to Venice we find a contrast striking and powerful. The philosophy of Venetian painting makes it almost a distinct

135

art from Florentine, for a picture to the one meant something altogether different from a picture to the other. A picture to a Florentine meant a skilfully drawn figure or combination of figures with color enough to give it the appearance of life, color as an element being always subordinated to form. To a Venetian, on the contrary, a picture meant a skilful combination of colors with form enough to give it the appearance of nature, form being always subordinated to color. The especial significance of his reciprocal relation of form and color will be treated later.

Of the social life of Venice during the period of her prosperity, we have picture after picture in the chroniclers and poets of the time. Her name stood to other nations for three things in particular: wealth, licentious luxury, and pride, the latter shading off into cruelty. Through her commerce all nations paid her tribute. Spices from Arabia, silks from China, amber from the Baltic, pearls from the Persian Gulf might be found together in one street in Venice and in Venice alone of all the cities of the world. Her wealth contributed to make her proud and haughty. Mysterious dungeons of the Ten into which unhappy prisoners disappeared by night to be seen no more, torture chambers below the level of the Adriatic where forsaken wretches found relief in death, red columns of the Ducal Palace between which the lifeless bodies of the condemned, swaying in the wind, might be seen by the merchantmen anchored in the port—all of these things told stories of the horrible scenes enacted there and of her cruelty matched only by her pride. As to the licentiousness of her private life not only history but literature bears ample testimony. *Volpone or the Fox,* one of the greatest comedies ever written, portrays, with all the strength and fire with which its author, Ben Jonson, was capable, the degeneracy of Venice. Shakspere in *Othello* has illustrated the same thing. The damning consciousness that Desdemona would only be true to the instincts of her own people in being unfaithful, as Iago suggests, is one of the chief reasons why Othello is convinced that Iago speaks the truth. The conscience of Venice, he says, is not to keep from doing evil but to keep from being found out after the evil is done, and Othello from his own observation recognizes the truth of this. The vice of Venice was not a casual thing, but a part of the constitution of society and the state. Hers was not the Roman coarseness or the Greek softness and ease, but rather the Assyrian splendor of the purple magnificence in which Tyre clothed her sin. The life of Venice was one perpetual round of pleasure and gaiety. All that art could devise to throw a halo around the sensual appeal was present in her elaborate balls and banquets, which were a part of her nightly revelries. Byron in the fourth act of *Marino Faliero* and Browning in *A Toccata of Galuppi's* have brought the scene more vividly before us. All that the beauty of the material could produce, the most exquisite physical charms, the richness of flowers and perfumes, the brilliancy of countless jewels, the fairy fabrics of glass, an art which still excites the wonder of the world, the gorgeously colored frescoes—what a setting for all the revelry, what a picture of the Bride of the Sea! Browning's *A Toccata of Galuppi's,* a few stanzas of which I quote below, gives a very vivid picture of her wealth and voluptuousness:

"Here you come with your old music, and here's all the good it brings.
  What, they lived once thus at Venice where the merchants were the
      kings,
  Where St. Mark's is, where the Doges used to wed the sea with
      rings?

"Did young people take their pleasure when the sea was warm in
      May?
  Balls and masks begun at midnight, burning ever to mid-day,
  When they made up fresh adventures for the morrow, do you say?

"Was a lady such a lady, cheeks so round and lips so red,—
On her neck the small face buoyant, like a bell-flower on its bed,
O'er the breast's superb abundance where a man might base his head?

"As for Venice and her people, merely born to bloom and drop,
Here on earth they bore their fruitage, mirth and folly were the
    crop:
What of soul was left I wonder when the kissing had to stop?"

It was as the final expression of such a people and such ideals that we must study the work of Titian of Cadore, who in himself summed up the art of his nation and in his own way expressed her ideals.   He lived to be the oldest of all the painters, so old in fact that he did not seem to be quite sure himself how old he was.   From his own statement as to the date of his birth he was within a few months of being one hundred years of age when he died.   His long life was one of activity, and yet he accomplished very little compared with Raphael, who died at thirty-seven.

In personal traits Titian embodied completely the characteristics of his people.   He was the most avaricious of all the Italian painters, not excepting Pietro Perugino, and out of the long correspondence between him and Charles V. and his son there is scarcely a letter which does not ask for money.   He wrote to the former, acknowledging a pension of 500 *scudi,* which the Emperor had just given him, that he needed money.   "I have been in ill health," he says, "and having married a daughter am straitened for means."   The health statement may have been correct, though he lived to be a hundred, but the reference to his daughter's marriage to speak mildly was a prevarication.   The date of the letter is September 10, 1554, and as his only daughter was not married until the year 1555, she could not have been married when he wrote the letter.   At another time he wrote to Philip complaining that he had not been paid in gold, although the latter had just sent him 2000 *scudi*.   At still another he writes:

"Meanwhile I beg your majesty most humbly and out of old friendship before I die to do me the grace to give me some consolation and utility of the privilege of corn from Naples which was granted to me so long ago by the Caesar of glorious memory, your majesty's progenitor. I beg likewise to ask for some pension."

His fondness for money was matched by the customary Venetian indifference to moral restraints. He was married, but according to his own testimony the ceremony was only performed because of legal considerations. He was a member of the dissolute triumvirate to which Pietro Aretino, the greatest blackmailer in the history of the world, and the profligate, though brilliant sculptor, Sansovino, belonged, although Titian seems to have been the least extreme of the three. However, in spite of all his moral lapses he was kind and considerate to his family. His oldest son, whom he wanted to be a priest, turned out a reprobate and spent all the money he could get from his father. His daughter Lavinia was his favorite child, whom he has portrayed frequently on canvas. She was a beautiful girl, though her face, in the Dresden picture, has an expression one would rather not see there. She married at the age of twenty-four and died two years later. One thinks more of Lavinia and infinitely more of Titian if he does not believe the authenticity of the title of the Dresden picture, especially after he has seen the *Venus* of the Uffizi.

Titian was born about 1476 or 1477 at Cadore, a little town, near the Alps, belonging to the city of Venice. His memory about this first event in his life was never accurate. After the first ten years of his career, which were spent in his native place, he was sent to Venice to learn the art of painting. There he came under the influence of the Bellini brothers, about whose work Ruskin displays such epileptic admiration. John Bellini could paint religious subjects with almost as much fervor as that sublime rascal, Pietro Perugino, and was far and away the better artist. Ruskin thinks that John Bellini has painted a Madonna which has more religion, and at the same time more art about it, than any other picture in the world. If this distinguished critic is right,—I think the accuracy of his criticism may be challenged—it gives Bellini's Madonna precedence over the *Granduca* and the *Sistine*. However this may be, Titian was learning from John Bellini, and at the age of twenty painted a picture, now in the gallery of Antwerp, of Jacopo Pesaro doing homage to St. Peter. Pesaro, who has just won a great victory over the Turks, is kneeling before the apostle presenting his banner, while the fat, bloated and sensual Alexander Borgia, who filled the papal throne at the time, is standing a little in the background introducing Jacopo to Peter, while the latter seems to be acknowledging the introduction. Under the platform on which Peter is sitting are nude mythological figures not easily understood, until it is remembered that in those times religion and mythology were, in the minds of most people, so hopelessly mixed up that poets were uncertain as to whether they should dedicate their poems to Venus or Mary. There is a very peculiar expression on Peter's face. He seems ill at ease before the Pope in his tiara and robes and looks as if his distinguished successor to the papal chair has come at an inopportune and unexpected moment, though one would think that Peter would not be abashed or embarrassed even in the presence of a Borgia. There is a serio-comical expression on the face of the Pope which contrasts strangely with the alarm of Peter and the ridiculously inane features of Jacopo, who grasps the flagstaff with both hands and thrusts the banner itself directly in the Pope's face. It is not a great picture, but interesting because it is about the earliest painting of any importance known to have been done by Titian.

It was in these early days of his career that he became acquainted with Giorgione, the first of the quartet of great Venetian painters, Titian himself, Tintoretto and Paul of Verona being the other three. He was preeminently the poet of the Venetian school and put more soul into his work than any of the others. His life was a romantic one and terminated abruptly at the age of thirty-two. According to Vasari his early death was due to his devoted attachment to a young girl whom he refused to leave during her illness with fever, thus falling a victim to the same disease. According to other authorities he died of chagrin because a friend won the affections of the same girl.

Of Giorgione's work, specimens of which may be seen in Dresden, in the Louvre, and in Florence, it may be said that in richness of tone, sympathetic feeling and idealization of the flesh, an ideal which Titian rarely, if ever, reached, he marks the high water level of the Venetian school. There is one picture attributed to him—some recent authorities have been trying to give it to Titian—which is the finest thing of the kind in the world, and once seen is never forgotten. It is the *Concert,* now in the first room of the Pitti Gallery in Florence. It represents the effect of music upon a group of three persons. Two Augustine monks have just finished playing a duet, the fingers of one still resting upon the instrument while he looks at his companion with an expression, such as the world cannot parallel, of complete absorption in the music, the last notes of which have just ceased reverberating in the room. One feels that Browning, to whom that room was as familiar as his own home, must have written *Abt Vogler* after seeing the *Concert.* The man whose large, soulful eyes look out of this picture and whose wonderfully delicate fingers rest upon the keys is not in or of this world at all; he belongs to that transcendent land into which Abt Vogler has gone, mounting up on the wings of music or bringing this world down to him, as Browning's poem discloses:

"In sight? Not half! for it seemed, it was certain, to match man's
      birth,
Nature in turn conceived, obeying an impulse as I;
And the emulous heaven yearned down, made effort to reach the
      earth,
As the earth had done her best, in my passion to scale the sky:
Novel splendors burst forth, grew familiar and dwelt with mine,
Not a point nor peak but found and fixed its wandering star;
Meteor-moons, balls of blaze: and they did not pale nor pine,
For earth had attained to heaven, there was no more near nor far.

"Nay more: for there wanted not who walked in the glare and the
      glow,
Presences plain in the place; or, fresh from the Protoplast,
Furnished for ages to come, when a kindlier wind should blow
Lured now to begin and live, in a house to their liking at last;
Or else the wonderful Dead who have passed through the body and
      gone,
But were back once more to breathe in an old world worth their new:
What never had been was now; what was, as it shall be anon;
And what is,—shall I say, matched both? for I was made perfect
      too.

"Therefore to whom turn I but to thee, the ineffable Name?
Builder and maker, thou, of houses not built with hands!
What, have fear of change from thee who art ever the same?
Doubt that thy power can fill the heart that thy power expands?
There shall never be one lost good! What was, shall live as before;
Evil is null, is naught, is silence implying sound;
What was good shall be good, with, for evil, so much good more;
On earth the broken arcs; in the heaven a perfect round.

"All we have willed or hoped or dreamed of good shall exist;
Not its semblance, but itself; no beauty, nor good, nor power
Whose voice has gone forth, but each survives for the melodist
When eternity confirms the conception of an hour.
The high that proved too high, the heroic for earth too hard,
The passion that left the ground to lose itself in the sky,
Are music sent up to God by the lover and the bard;
Enough that he heard it once; we shall hear it by and by."

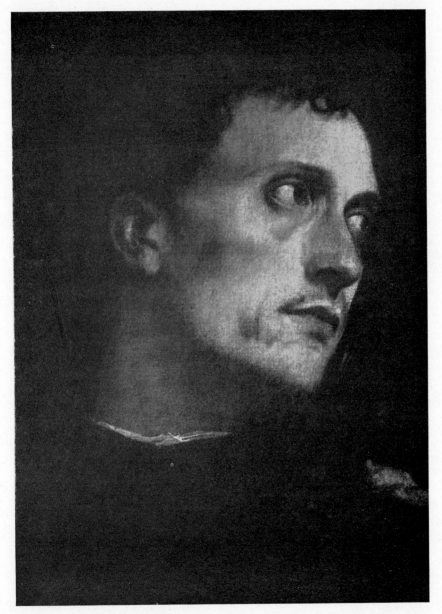

Detail of the Concert   *Florence*

By Giorgione

All this and more the one monk sees in his transfiguration. The other monk, an older man, who is also deeply affected by the music, does not seem to possess that delicacy of feeling which enables him to enter into the emotional depths of his companion. The third figure in the group is a young man gayly and jauntily dressed in an orange-colored jacket and wearing a cap with white feathers. He is not interested in the music but seems to be waiting for his two companions to return to the earth. The coloring of the picture is excellent and the harmony throughout superb. The *Concert* is perhaps the greatest music picture in existence, and it is most unfortunate that we do not know with any assurance who painted it. Until recently it was universally conceded to be Giorgione's and Walter Pater in his work on the school of Giorgione makes it the central picture in his discussion of that painter, but recent authorities, one after another, disagree with Pater.

Titian's life as an artist may be divided into three periods: the first, or early division extending from 1476 to 1513, is the period of the Giorgione influence; the second, distinguished by greater realism, breadth and color and by a falling off in the semi-spiritual quality of his early work, extends from 1513 to 1530; the third, distinguished by the complete dominance of color in his treatment of objects and by a colder realism than that which marks his second period, extends from 1530 to the close of his life.

During Titian's first period, when his work was modeled on Giorgione's and, as a consequence, has more soul in it than there is in his later productions, he painted, beside the *Concert* (if the latter picture can be correctly attributed to him), three others which are characteristic, two of which are doubtless the greatest pictures he ever produced. They are the *Three Ages of Man* in the Bridgewater Gallery, *The Tribute Money* at Dresden and the *Sacred and Profane*

Love in the Borghese Gallery in Rome. The first represents three groups of figures set in a beautiful country environment. At the right of the picture a shepherd and shepherdess, the latter with a garland of flowers in her hair, are seated, the man holding the woman in his arms, who is playing a lute, while at the left there is a group of children. In the centre, at some distance from each of the other groups, an old man stands surrounded by a row of skulls which he is contemplating. It is the same story which has been told many times in poetry and literature, but never more beautifully embodied than in Titian's picture. The young man and maiden are conscious only of love and the music, to both of which they surrender themselves unreservedly. The children play on unconscious of the future. The old man looks into the grave and anticipates the time when his own skull will join earth's caravan of skulls. To elaborate upon the symbolism of this picture is unnecessary.

The Tribute Money at Dresden is the best religious picture Titian ever painted. The face of Christ in this painting has been regarded by some enthusiasts as equal to that of Leonardo's in the *Last Supper,* and as far as the purely human element is concerned they are probably right; but with all of its real nobility the face is hardly one which we should involuntarily worship. There is something lacking, something which Titian could not put there, though it must be admitted that he came nearer doing it here than anywhere else. The conception is splendid; the contrast between the noble face of the Christ and the scheming, malignant countenance of the Herodian is one of the most striking in all the round of pictorial art. Why, it may be asked, does this face represent the highest level Titian ever reached in portraying religious feeling? The answer is that here the idealistic or spiritual quality, which gives life to the work of Giorgione, is still present. Later, in working out the Venetian ideal of color, Titian sinks to a decidedly materialistic level. Yet at its best the Christ of Titian is never the Christ of Leonardo. Only the greatest genius of modern times could paint that face, and so far as depth of thought is concerned Titian is as far from Leonardo as the horizon from the zenith.

Of all these pictures none are quite so famous as his *Sacred and Profane Love* in the Borghese Gallery. This painting was sold to the Italian Government a few years ago for approximately two hundred thousand dollars. There has been more controversy over this picture than any or all of the other Titians put together. Which is Sacred and which is Profane Love? Is the name authentic at all? If not, what ought it to be called? These are some of the questions which the traveler hears as he draws near the Borghese Gallery. The details of the picture are simple enough. Two young women, the one richly dressed in splendid raiment, wearing a red girdle fastened with a rich, jewelled clasp at the waist, the other in the lightest possible drapery, are seated on the edge of a fountain, while a mischievous little Cupid plays in the water. The undraped figure looks with artless innocence at her richly clad companion, who, gazing primly before her, does not return the look. In the first reference to the picture, about 1648, it was called *Two Maidens at a Fountain*. Later, it was given its present name. The commonly accepted opinion is that the draped figure represents Sacred Love and the undraped figure Profane Love; but there seems to be so much that is not sacred about the one which has been adjudged sacred that a schism in interpretation has resulted, a large number of critics reversing their opinion and claiming that it is Profane Love which needs and wears the drapery, while Sacred Love requires no external adornment. The controversy finally grew so ardent, and became such a mere war of words, that the controversialists themselves at last grew weary of the fruitless argument and came even to doubt the accuracy of the title itself. Leaders in art criticism came from all over the world to lay their offering on the altar of words. Messieurs Crowe and Cavalcaselle, who certainly stand first in aught having to do with the history of art, triumphantly labeled the picture *Artless and Sated Love*. They proceeded to show that the draped figure by her look of disgust, by the faded rose at her feet, by even the insert sculptured on the fountain, could represent only the sated feelings of *ennui* which love may and does often come to possess, while the undraped figure, in her look of innocence and inexperience, testifies to the artlessness of untried affection. This theory, however, was accepted by no one. Another critic, Franz Wickhoffe, a German, scenting a flavor of antiquity about the theme, discovered forthwith in the seventh book of the *Argonautica* of Valerius Flaccus, an imitation of *The Argonauts* of Apollonius Rhodius, some lines refering to the story of Medea which would identify the famous Colchian sorceress, who refused to marry Jason, the enemy of her people, with Sacred Love, while Venus, who urges Medea to perform the marriage rites, is Profane Love. This interpretation was the one most generally favored. It has the advantage of being classic, and Sacred Love does indisputably have a slightly Medea-like cast; the honor, therefore, so far belongs to Herr Wickhoffe and the *Argonautica* of Valerius Flaccus, though it is to be very seriously doubted whether this, or any, theory will settle the controversy.

Sacred and Profane Love is the most complete representative painting of Titian's early or Giorgionesque period. It is now his most popular picture, and certainly one of his most beautiful. In his early days he was at times more than the Venetian, and rose above the purely materialistic ideal. About 1513 he emancipated himself from Giorgione's influence and struck out on more distinctive lines.

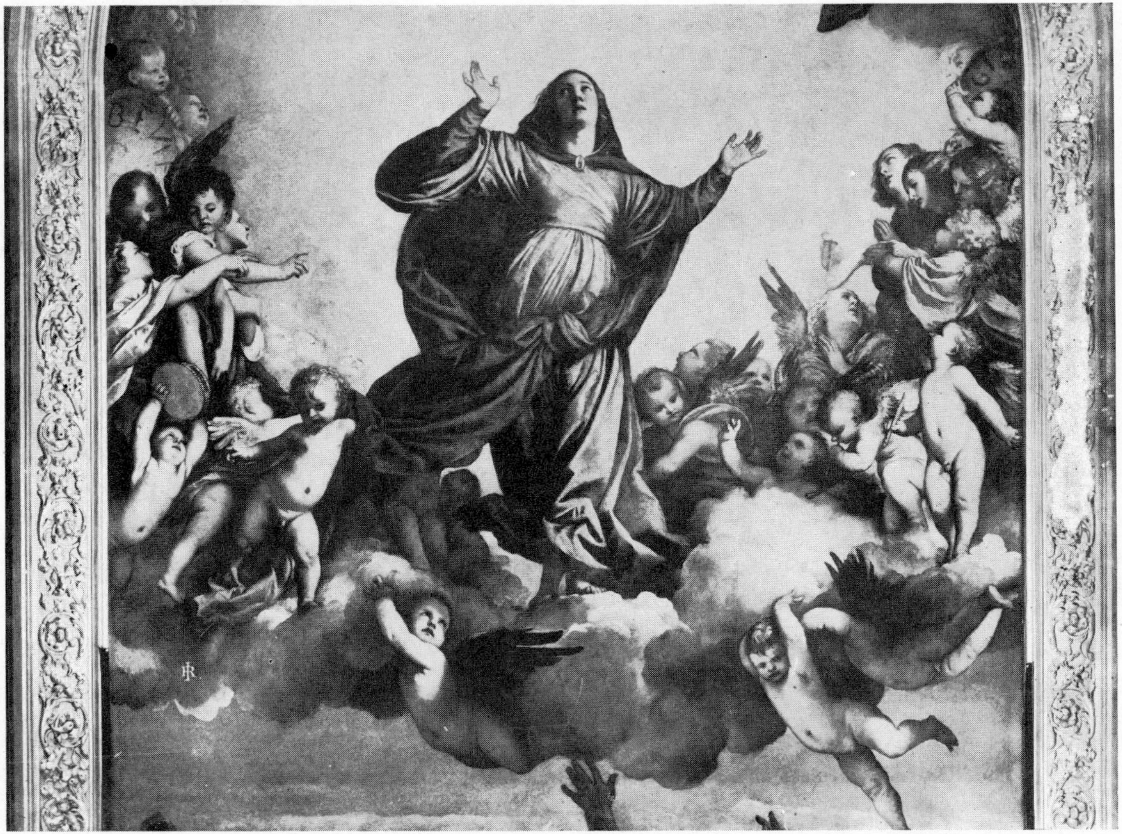

The Assumption — *The Academy, Venice*

By Titian

From now on his technique shows marked improvement, the chief feature of which is the use he makes of the element of action, something which hitherto his figures do not have. His coloring also improved and he became decidedly more realistic. It was in this period that he painted some of his greatest church pictures, among them being the deservedly world-famous *Assumption, St. Peter Martyr,* by some critics regarded as his greatest painting and which is now destroyed, the *Noli me Tangere* in the National Gallery and the *Pesaro Madonna* in Venice. Among his secular pictures are *Bacchus and Ariadne, Flora,* and sundry Venuses, the one especially in the Bridgewater Gallery, in London.

The *Assumption,* which hangs in the Academy in Venice, and which has the greatest reputation of any in that city, is listed as one of the twelve World Pictures. Many people are enraptured over the divine expression and transcendent beauty of the Virgin's face; but with the utmost consideration for their feeling and judgment I can see no divinity, not even transcendent beauty there. As a religious picture it is inferior to *The Tribute Money,* but as a piece of technique it is unquestionably great, and as a masterpiece of color it may be called transcendent. What pen can describe that sea of golden light in which Mary floats upward to the heavens, borne on the billows of massive clouds which cast their shadows on the earth! It is entrancingly, wondrously beautiful, but it is an earthly not a divine beauty. What a vast difference there is between this gorgeous incarnation of red and gold and blue and the frescoes of the Sistine Chapel, or the *Sistine Madonna* or the *Last Supper* at Milan! Here we have the Venetian and the Tuscan side by side, and among art lovers and critics there is no dispute as to which should receive the crown.

Titian's *Pesaro Madonna* is one of the most peculiarly constructed pictures in the world. The plan of this painting provided for three things: first, Jacopo Pesaro and his banner, second St. Peter, and third, Mary and Christ. How the artist was to get these three objects in without making the picture ridiculous and at the same time how he was to flatter Pesaro sufficiently to guarantee the payment of the stipulated sum for the painting, was a problem. But the great artist mastered the difficult situation. He painted, as a background, two tremendous pillars with a bit of magnificent Venetian sky between them, enthroning the virgin and the child immediately in front of the left pillar, placing St. Peter between the pillars and immortalizing Pesaro and his banner at the right corner of the picture, both on a diagonal line below the virgin and child. By this arrangement Titian made Mary the center of interest, though she is not in the centre of the picture and does not occupy as much space as St. Peter or Pesaro's banner. The color scheme was apparently made to contribute to the same end. Mary is clothed in a white veil with the sunlight shining directly upon her. Peter is arrayed in blue and gold and catches the eye immediately after Mary. He attires Jacopo in the most magnificent suit of black satin that a painter ever made from oils and pigments, and though its color tends to lessen the prominence of Pesaro, it, at the same time, by its appropriateness and richness, leaves him nothing of which to complain. The *Pesaro Madonna* hangs in the church of the Ferari in Venice and is a picture of great interest, especially after its history is known.

The *St. Peter Martyr,* painted for the church of St. Giovanni and Paolo in Venice, and destroyed by fire in 1867, was the most dramatic of all the pictures of Titian and was considered his best. In this painting Titian was supposed to have imitated Michael Angelo, and from the accounts of those who saw it the painting deserved its reputation. The picture shows Peter attacked and killed by robbers in a lonely wood and the countenance of the Saint as he struggles helplessly on the ground and the fierce and murderous expression on the faces of his assailants are superbly drawn even in the copies. The coloring in this picture was equal to Titian's best work, which is saying a great deal.

It is in his mythological and classical pictures, however, that we see Titian at his best. In the *Bacchus and Ariadne*, which Ruskin said was the most valuable in the National Gallery, where it hangs, the spirit of materialism, which is incarnate in his works, finds full and complete expression. Very beautiful indeed is the god, his red robes floating in the sunlight, as he alights from his leopard-drawn car to greet Ariadne, who, fleeing from this god of the chalice, turns to look back. In color arrangement and in the emphasis laid upon action we are far away from the days of the *Sacred and Profane Love*. Titian's materialistic tendency is best shown, however, in his Venuses, the *Venus* arising from the sea in the Bridgewater collection being one of the most beautiful, although a long way below the Profane Love. Whatever beauty earth and earth alone possesses it has, but no more. This tendency to lower the dignity of womanly beauty to a level no higher than the material, was carried out by Titian in later years in the numerous Venuses, Danaes and Antiopes which have filled Europe with his name. Titian once told Aretino that he had "never seen a maiden without discovering in her features a touch of sensuality," and his whole conception of womanhood never rose above that level. It is quite true that no painter has ever succeeded in making material beauty more attractive than he or in bringing out the best it has to give, but, after all, most people prefer to let their thoughts linger with the *Sistine Madonna* or the wistful faces of Botticelli, which speak of something nobler and higher. And yet Titian's goddesses are beautiful, and there is something divine in beauty even though it be of clay; were it not for this fact he had long since passed into oblivion instead of taking his place with the giants of Tuscany.

The best that is in these earthly beautiful women comes out in his *Flora* in the Uffizi Gallery in Florence. She is the loveliest girl face he ever painted. Her features are as perfect as the imagination can make them. The long curling hair which falls over a perfect neck and shoulders, the divine tints of the cheeks, the soft lashes of her eyes, the exquisitely moulded chin, all these must and do give pleasure to any one who cares for beauty at all. It is when we look into Flora's eyes that we feel a lack of something, a loss, a disappointment; they are perfect and full of expression, but it is the expression of mere animal pleasure, not indeed the soulless look of Lucrezia del Fede but the naive glance of a child. Somehow we expect something better of Lucrezia and are angry when we do not obtain it, but who could expect anything more of Flora? She is a little woodland nymph who belongs to the earth alone; she is very beautiful, very charming just as she is, and no one would wish her—cannot think of her—otherwise. But in spite of all her beauty and charm the mind irresistibly goes back to the *Mona Lisa,* and we see and feel the difference between the two women, discerning, as we have never done before, the difference between the glory of the ideal and the glory of the material. "There is one glory of the sun and another glory of the moon and another glory of the stars, and one star differeth from another in glory." And in like manner does the glory of Leonardo differ from the glory of Titian.

The final period of Titian's life as an artist began about 1530. This is also the year of his wife's death and his change of residence to a beautiful home in North Venice, where he laid out an attractive garden which reminded him no doubt of the beautiful mountains around his old home at

Cadore. Here he entertained his friends, among others the famous blackmailer Aretino, to whom reference has already been made. Aretino was so outrageously caustic, untruthful and scurrilous and so clever in his colossal meanness that to escape his slanderous pen, nearly every prominent person in Christendom paid him tribute. This he called "living by the sweat of his pen." He "was cursed," it is recorded, "with inordinate desires of every kind." His appetites of the senses were almost insatiable. He liked dinners, dress and high company, varied on occasions with the lowest forms of debauch. Like a fungus which thrives on decaying vegetable matter, he lived and battened upon the general corruption of the time. He tried to levy contributions upon Michael Angelo who refused to be bulldozed, whereupon Aretino addressed him a letter in which he so artfully and insidiously slandered him that his one letter did more damage to the great painter's character than all other things put together. The death of Aretino in 1556 was very unusual. It occurred about three o'clock in the morning while he was indulging in one of his orgies in his palace on the Grand Canal. A guest told a joke which caused the cynic to laugh so immoderately that he lost his balance and fell from his chair striking his head against an object in the room. His death resulted almost immediately, but he lived long enough to receive extreme unction. He died, as he had lived, a blasphemer. His last words to the priest were: "Now that I am oiled keep me from the rats!" This much has been written about Pietro Aretino because, for nearly thirty years, he was Titian's most intimate associate.

During the concluding period of his life the painter came into that active association with the great European monarchs of the house of Hapsburg which constitutes one of the most interesting events of his career. Some of his best pictures had been painted for the Duke of Ferrara and

for Francesco Maria della Rovere, Duke of Urbino, but not
until two years after the death of his wife did he meet Charles
V., Emperor of Germany, at that time the most powerful
monarch in Europe. Charles was so well pleased with
Titian's skill that he employed him as his court painter, con-
ferring upon him the title of Count Palatine, at the same
time raising his children to the rank of nobles of the empire
with all the honors belonging to families with four generations of ancestors. Titian himself was made a Knight of the
Golden Spur and allowed free entrance to the Court at any
time. Better than all else, perhaps, to the Venetian was the
thousand *scudi* in gold which the Emperor bestowed upon
him every time he painted his picture, which was done as
frequently as could be managed, we can safely affirm, knowing as well as we do the character of Titian in relation to
money.

From this time on Titian painted portraits until he
became one of the foremost, if not the very greatest, portrait
painter that ever lived. His likenesses were true to life, but
he always chose the most favorable attitude and employed
the most artistic disposition of light and shade and the most
skilful combinations of color possible for his work. As an
example of this his picture of Charles' son, Philip the Second, one of the ugliest monarchs in every respect that ever
disgraced the world, was so toned down that Mary, Queen
of England, fell in love with the picture to such a degree
that even the disenchantment of the original could not
destroy her love for it. From a description of Philip given
by a contemporary it was no little achievement of Titian to
paint a likeness of such a model making him fairly good
looking and at the same time true to life, withal constituting
out of the picture, as a whole, a work of art.

During the last period of his life, Titian's family of
Venuses, already numerous, increased until nearly every

Portrait of Catharine Cornaro   *Florence*
By Titian

monarch in Europe had one or more of them. Philip himself ordered a large number. The best in every respect of all his classical or mythological pictures is the *Jupiter and Antiope* in the Louvre. There is in it a touch of the poetry of his early Giorgione work, but the situation itself hopelessly destroys the ideal element. Were Antiope alone, just as she is portrayed, the whole picture would be an infinitely higher creation. The materializing tendency, present in all of these pictures, comes to full flowering in works like the *Danae* in Naples and the *Europa* owned by Mrs. Gardner of Boston. In these pictures there is no expression above the sensual; they are below even the Greek level of idealism in the same way that the purple vice of Tyre and Sidon was below the free ideas of Athens and Ephesus on social questions. Whatever apologists for Titian may say the fact remains that in such creations as these he not only becomes a spokesman of a vicious theory of life, but just as surely becomes an apostle of a false ideal of art. What infinite distances there are between the *Mona Lisa* and the *Profane Love,* and what equally infinite distances between the *Profane Love* and the *Europa.* The one is a descent from the divine to the human, the other is a descent from the human to the brute. I yield to no one in my belief that art and ethics have separate realms and that art questions and ethical questions are distinct, but art of this kind is not really beautiful and is therefore not art in the real and true sense.

Along with portraits and realistic mythological pictures, Titian painted a number of sacred subjects during this long concluding period of his life which show even more conclusively than his Venuses and Antiopes the deadening influence of the materialistic ideal. Three, out of a large number, will serve to exemplify the correctness of this statement. These are the *Magdalen* in the Pitti Gallery in Florence, the *Ecce Homo* in Vienna and the *Christ Crowned with Thorns* in the Louvre.

The Magdalen has always been a favorite subject with painters, and during my residence in Florence I collected several dozen different conceptions of the subject of Italian painters alone. Generally speaking, there are five types of womanhood represented in Italian art: first, the innocence of girlhood embodied in pictures of the Virgin prior to the annunciation; second, the dignity of motherhood, after the birth of Christ, represented in the Madonnas; third, the repentant type portrayed in the Magdalens; fourth, the pure Venus type borrowed from the Greeks, a frank idealization of the best that is in a purely material conception of womanhood; and fifth, a lower Venus type, an idealization of what may be called the sensual side of the Material, exemplified in Titian's *Europa* and *Danae*. From the Magdalen ideal have come many beautiful pictures, not the least attractive of which is Domenichino's splendid representation in the Pitti Gallery. There is as much difference between the painting of Domenichino and Titian's in the same gallery as there is between light and darkness. Bayard Taylor, who saw Titian's *Magdalen* when a mere boy, made the naive though just criticism that the picture did not seem to him like a Magdalen weeping tears of repentance for her sin, but like a woman mourning over an absent lover. A more complete failure to realize a comparatively easy ideal for a Tuscan cannot be imagined. The coloring—the one thing in which Titian never failed—in this picture is superb; but color can no more portray a Magdalen than it can portray a Christ. The *Ecce Homo* and the *Christ Crowned with Thorns* exemplify this fact.

The *Ecce Homo* is one of the largest of Titian's canvases. In coloring, in the splendid grouping and arrangement of figures in dramatic action, it is a great picture.

But what a travesty is the face of the Christ! One cannot but inquire what has become of the noble Christ face of *The Tribute Money* of forty years before? Christ has also been dragged down to the level of the material and he who can see one spark of divinity, or even a high type of manhood in it, must possess more imagination than the artist himself.

The *Christ Crowned with Thorns* was originally painted for the church of Santa Marie della Grazie of Milan, in the refectory of which hangs the *Last Supper* of Leonardo. The expression here is as feeble as in the *Ecce Homo,* possibly more so. Of all imaginable contrasts none can be greater than that between the face in this picture and the face of the one who has just uttered "One of you shall betray me" in Leonardo's. Here again we have the Spirit of the Ideal and the Spirit of the Material in immediate juxtaposition. The *Christ Crowned with Thorns* has been transferred to the Louvre, while the *Last Supper* remains in lonely and solitary grandeur and ruin, the guardian genius of Milan.

Of all the work of Titian's later years we like best to dwell upon his portraits of his daughter Lavinia, a number of which are scattered over Europe. Perhaps the most interesting is the one in Berlin which represents her holding a dish of fruit in her hand. Titian's love for her is one of the brightest spots in his life. The ideality of a father's affection remains his in any event and a love which the materialism of Venice could not entirely destroy. The most distinctive thing about the handsome *La Bella* in the Pitti, the alleged mistress of Titian, is the color. Never before did a woman's clothes constitute such an important factor in a picture. Proud and sensual as she looks, the painter's emphasis upon her attire tells her character better perhaps than it could be portrayed in any other way. La Bella's face is found in many of Titian's pictures.

Titian's last painting was a *Pieta* which he never finished. Raphael died leaving unfinished his great *Transfiguration,* the sublimest object ever given to man to show how the material can be transfigured by the glory of the ideal. Titian died leaving also an unfinished picture, his being a scene of the saddest and most hopeless moment in the history of Christianity, a moment in which it seemed that, after all, dust and ashes were the destiny of human life, for the dead Christ had not yet risen. Once more, in these last two pictures, both unfinished, we have the contrast of the opposing tendencies of the two masters who best exemplified the ideal and material in their works, the one picture representing the risen Christ transfigured by a light which never yet had shone upon the land or sea, the other representing the cold, unresponsive material form of the dead Jesus.

Titian died on August 27, 1576, while the plague was raging in Venice, though it is not known whether he was a victim of this terrible scourge or not. He was buried with honor in the church of the Ferari where his tomb, marked by a monument of later date, remains to this day.

His paintings, of which one hundred and sixty-three are catalogued, are scattered all over the world. There are fourteen in Austria, seventeen in England, approximately twenty-four in France, fourteen in Florence, twenty-one in Venice and twenty-six in Madrid, the latter city being the best place to study Titian's later style. To observe his earlier manner a student should go to Rome, Florence and Venice. His pictures may be conveniently studied under the three-fold division of Religious, Classical and Mythological, and Portraits. The most representative of the first division are the *Assumption,* the *St. Peter Martyr,* the *Pesaro Madonna,* the *Presentation in the Temple,* the *Ecce Homo,* and the unfinished *Pieta;* of the second are the *Sacred and Profane Love,* the *Three Ages of Man,* the *Bacchus and*

Ariadne, the *Jupiter and Antiope,* the Venuses in the Uffizi
and Bridgewater collections and the *Danae* at Naples; of
the third are the idealized portraits of *The Man with the
Glove* in the Louvre, the *La Bella,* the *Flora* and the royal
portraits of Charles and Philip, to which we might add those
of the Duke and Duchess of Urbino; nor to this list should
we fail to include the Lavinia portraits at Berlin and Dresden. Very many others of equal value and importance might
be catalogued but it is safe to say that any one who knows
these paintings will know Titian at his best.

In Leonardo we found the incarnation of the intellectual ideal in art, and the conception that the mystery of
woman's personality holds all other problems in solution.
In Botticelli we found the incarnation of the soul's unrest,
its dissatisfaction with the actual and its longing for the
ideal. In Michael Angelo we saw transcendent epic power
and towering sublimity, with a superb appeal to masculine
strength in nature and art. In Raphael we discovered the incarnations of the supreme glory of ideal motherhood and the
idealization of the highest type of human love and sympathy
with ideal purity and beauty, reaching the culmination of
the message that painting can bring to man. In Andrea
del Sarto we found the tragedy of genius, springing from
his devotion to a low ideal which destroys human effort and
makes great and lofty achievements impossible. At the last
we find Titian, embodying the interpretation of the purely
material, expressed preeminently in color. This closes the
survey of Italian painting, the greatest and most glorious
body of plastic form and color ever achieved. In all the
realms of poetry and history sublimer . lessons than are
taught here, can scarcely be found. Because of all these
things our study has been made more from the standpoint
of the message than from the technical excellencies, *per se,*
or the historical events in the lives of the painters themselves.

It is fitting that the last word of this study should be in reference to the materialism of color which dominates Titian's work. Color is essentially allied to materialism as form is to idealism. Why this is true cannot be explained here. Suffice it to say that it is a fact that they are so allied. Color has everywhere in history and art tended toward a material and sensual ideal, and form, from the days of Plato, toward a spiritual ideal. Titian's devotion to color resulted in the embodiment of Venetian luxury and life, and we have seen how, as he became more and more devoted to it, he lost his sense of ideal verities. Materialism doubtless has its charms, and yet what a tragedy it seems when we compare the *Sistine Madonna,* for example, with the *Antiope* in the Louvre; both women, transcendently beautiful, but the gulf that is between them! When I think of the lovely physical form of Antiope or Danae and then of Mary of Dresden, I am reminded irresistibly of Coventry Patmore's words:

> "Ah! wasteful woman; she who may
> On her sweet self set her own price,
> Knowing he cannot choose but pay,
> How has she cheapened Paradise,
> How given for naught her priceless gift,
> How spoiled the bread and spilled the wine
> Which, spent with due respective thrift,
> Had made brutes, men; and men, divine."

The glory of Venice and the glory of Titian are of the kind that passes away. The banqueting chambers of Aretino are silent and empty; the beautiful women who sat for the great master have become dust and ashes; the music of their laughter is still; their wealth of silken hair and charms are no more. Peace be to them! and let them have what measure of immortality the genius of a Titian can give them.